February 2019

Joe... You obs[...] in [...] was
the homily the [...] Scripture,
one for the Eucharist, I add
that the homily, the Scripture
and the Eucharist prepare us
to fulfill the Great Commandment
... to be disciples, to be
light in a darkened world.
With hope, peace, and blessings
for your journey,

The Rhetoric of the Pulpit

The Rhetoric of the Pulpit

A Preacher's Guide to Effective Sermons

Jon Meyer Ericson

WIPF & STOCK · Eugene, Oregon

THE RHETORIC OF THE PULPIT
A Preacher's Guide to Effective Sermons

Wipf & Stock
An Imprint of Wipf and Stock Publishers
199 W. 8th Ave., Suite 3
Eugene, OR 97401

www.wipfandstock.com

PAPERBACK ISBN: 978-1-4982-3520-4
HARDCOVER ISBN: 978-1-4982-3522-8

Manufactured in the U.S.A.

To Pastors Jana and Marcus,

and to every other pastor or priest
whose delivery of the Word is a
beacon of light for a troubled world.

All author's royalties from the sale
of this book are dedicated to
seminary scholarships.

Contents

Chapter 3—Style: Effective Language Usage

Chapter 4—Delivery and Memory

Appendices

Acknowledgments

Thanks first to my dear wife, Amy, for all her patience through the long process of creating this book. And thanks to my former student Professor Don Boileau and to my friend Reverend David McMillan for their support and encouragement. Finally, a grateful author is thankful to Marcie McFall for putting the manuscript into a form the publisher could use.

Introduction

*Whoever speaks must do so as one speaking
the very words of God.*

1 Peter 4:11

IN THE BEGINNING WAS the Word, and now the articulation of the Word is in your hands. Joseph Sittler put it so clearly and so well as he observed that the pastor has the "stewardship of the mystery," is the "teller of that story."[1]

For most pastors, the sermon time is the most important fifteen or twenty minutes of the week, the time when the pastor is being pastor to the whole flock. It is also the time when newcomers and visitors are receiving an impression of who the pastor is. An underlying motivation for writing this book on the art of preaching is the belief that the Sunday sermon is the most important single factor in evangelism for a parish and also the most important factor in the spiritual growth of both the congregation and the pastor.

A second motivation is the conviction that rhetoric—the art of effective discourse—has much to offer the seminarian, and indeed, all who are entrusted with preaching the Word. An underlying assumption is that the preacher has had a good and thorough seminary preparation in the theological basis for sermon building, but probably has had little or no training in the rhetorical aspects. This lack of traditional rhetorical training in contemporary

1. Sittler, *Gravity and Grace*, 52

seminary curricula is a relatively new phenomenon, as we shall see as we review the historic relationship of rhetorical studies to preparation for the ministry, preparation for preaching.

The rhetorical aspects lead us to Greece and Italy, to Athens and Rome, the ground zero of classical rhetoric. Reference to the now ancient works of classical rhetoric is not made to provide an esoteric flavor to the text. Rather, the observation of the human phenomenon of communication made by Aristotle, Cicero, and Quintilian are indeed classic, timeless. St. Augustine, who has been identified as both "the last of the great ancient rhetoricians" and "the Church's foremost teacher in the classical art of Christian preaching"[2] turned to the rhetorical tradition of Greece and Rome to undergird the message written into his *De doctrina christiana* (On Christian doctrine), that pagan rhetoric had much to offer the church in the service of the truth. That the first three books of Augustine's enormously influential work focus on *the meaning of Scripture* and the fourth book on *how to communicate* the scriptural truths suggests another truth—that the Word, the spiritual aspects of preaching comes first. Rhetoric is always a *means*, always subordinate to the truth it serves.

As a personal note from one who has spent all of his adult life in the study of rhetoric, I want you to know that I see the subject not only as one of the oldest subjects of study in the world, but also one of the most interesting, intriguing, relevant, and challenging. Challenging because it is one of the most interdisciplinary, with close ties to logic, philosophy, history, sociology, psychology, and linguistics. It is no wonder that for nearly two hundred years Harvard, founded in 1638, devoted a full day a week to the study of rhetoric. The Boylston Chair of Rhetoric and Oratory was established at Harvard in 1806, with John Quincy Adams the first appointee. In contrast to the intensive study of rhetoric from the founding days of American universities, the study of English literature came 238 years later with Harvard's first appointment of a professor of English literature in 1876.

---

2. Johnson, "Isocrates Flowering," 217.

In short, the study of rhetoric and oratory has a long history and its strong companionship with preaching dates back at least as far as St. Augustine. Most recently, the relationship of rhetorical studies to Christian rhetoric is examined in the award-winning book *Mapping Christian Rhetorics*, a collection of scholarly research which demonstrates the importance of the Christian influence to rhetorical studies in general. Of interest to many would be their chapter titled, "'Heaven-Touched Lips and Pent-Up Voices': The Rhetoric of American Female Preaching Apologia, 1820–1930."[3]

Rhetoric, old and new, has always been a practical study, one that addresses the realities and circumstances of current issues and concerns as best they can be perceived. Rhetorical studies, knowledge of the communication process, is never more needed than now as we live in an information age threatening to drown us in a sea of words. While seeking certainties, we live in a rhetorical world of probabilities.

The traditional five divisions of rhetoric—Invention, Arrangement, Style, Memory, and Delivery—reflect a natural sequence of activity as one prepares a speech. First one must find the content, then organize it, then settle on the best words to express one's ideas, then actually deliver the content. The whole task of achieving effectiveness in the end product was the same for Demosthenes as it is for you. In sum, rhetorical theory, old and new, can be a useful guide to effective communication, effective sermons.

Accordingly, the aim here is to clarify and simplify the task of sermon preparation by presenting practical suggestions grounded in classical rhetorical theory as well as contemporary theories of communication. Clarifying and simplifying the preacher's task while providing a solid foundation should make the preacher comfortable and confident and profoundly influence the sermon's effectiveness.

To anyone who has listened to sermons over the decades, it is clear that there are many points of view on what the sermon should be. These range from the scholastic model with esoteric

---

3. DePalma and Ringer, *Mapping Christian Rhetorics*.

attention to the precise meaning of the words of the text to the stand-up entertainer who may leave the Word behind.

Most preachers will not be caught up in either of these extremes, but it is likely there will be uncertainty about the nature of the sermon and both tension and discomfort stemming from the difference between what the preacher thinks should be done and what he/she would actually like to do.

There are numerous wrong ideas about preaching. These include:

1. The pastor needs to come up with a great sermon every Sunday.

A great sermon is not possible each week, nor should it even be a goal. Do you even know what you mean by a *great sermon*? Do you set a standard for yourself based on the best preaching you have heard? While it is good to have models from which to learn, it is unwise and overly stressful to judge yourself in comparison to others. You have gifts which differ from others. Your sermon is *your sermon*. Gerhard Frost makes the point so well in his poem *Haunting Words*: "Yes, when you believe, and try to say what you believe, knowledge weds wisdom and heart language is born. Little words, feeling words, sturdy, simple words, strong-backed servants emerge to do Truth's bidding."[4]

A sermon is, first of all, a person speaking. The *great sermon* notion almost certainly places a wrong focus on the substance of the sermon, as if the product of the intellect were all that is involved in the communication process. The content is, indeed, an important and vital part of the rhetorical act we call the sermon, but it is just a part. The whole rhetorical act involves a person speaking, the speech, and an audience listening. The listeners are not expecting greatness, but they are expecting intimacy with both the Word and the pastor's response to the Word, and with the pastor's application of the Word to the listeners.

In sum, rather than seeking to present a great sermon, present *your sermon*. You are a particular person addressing a

4. Frost, *Blessed Is the Ordinary*, 61.

particular group of listeners on a particular text. Your listeners, your congregation, want to hear the explication of the Word from their pastor, to know his/her understanding, belief, feeling, and your application of the Word to them. So, trust yourself. Be yourself. Make the sermon your own.

2. Effective preaching requires a high degree of fluency in delivery.

While fluency is a positive aspect of delivery, it should not be overvalued. One can be too fluent so as to suggest slickness rather than thoughtfulness. Speakers who put too much stock in fluency may become overly dependent on extensive notes with whole sentences written out, or even become dependent on a manuscript. Either one is likely to become an obstacle to effective communication. As it is with the sermon as a whole . . . have the delivery be you, your sermon. Be yourself. The athlete, it is often said, is most effective when he/she "plays within himself." So, for the preacher: Be yourself. That is who the listeners want to hear.

3. Effective preaching requires more preparation time than the parish pastor can devote to the task.

Indeed, in his statement on what he expects of preachers, Pope Francis asks that they devote significant time to sermon preparation.[5] With the admonition to spend significant time in mind, I expect it will still come as a shock to you that the weekly preparation time recommended here is fifty-eight to sixty-two hours. That projection of hours spent in preparation is reasonable only if one acknowledges that the pastor is an especially endowed part of the creation with a brain which functions as a computer, but one which is never put to sleep. The process of preparation includes fifty-plus hours when the brain is working for you if you push the right buttons by downloading the text in a timely manner. That timely manner may differ in individual cases. While the schedule below suggests reviewing the text on Sunday evening, one of the most effective preachers I know has shared with me that

5. Pope Francis, *Evangelii Gaudium*, 156.

her preparation begins on Tuesday because she needs the interim time for refreshment and renewal.

So, while the specific practice of individuals will differ somewhat, the general idea in contemporary terms is to download the text early in your process of preparation. In the ancient terminology of both Joshua and the psalmist, "meditate day and night."

The process of preparation might follow a schedule something like this:

Day 1: Sunday at bedtime, and each evening at bedtime. Read and reread the texts for next Sunday. (In addition to you reading the texts, perhaps the easiest way to involve your congregation in Bible study is to include the texts for the *next* week in the Sunday's bulletin. The congregation will then have the opportunity to preview those texts . . . a good way to both create expectations and to stimulate both Bible reading and spiritual growth.)

Day 2: Monday, first thing. Read, peruse the texts. Begin making random notes on a large tablet. During the day, each day, ideas will come to you, wonderfully relevant materials will be remembered from your past experience and reading, and some current events will strike you as relevant to the texts. Be prepared to make notes on 3 x 5 cards or with whatever medium or technology is best for you.

Day 3: Tuesday. Spend an early hour with the text. Continue your notes and identify key ideas and supporting materials you may wish to use. Begin to think about the focus for the sermon, your specific *purpose* in relation to the lectionary texts.

Day 4: Wednesday, early hour or two. If you have not already chosen the specific text or texts you will use, settle on that now. In addition, this is the time to give thoughtful consideration to other texts which might help explicate or enrich the text for the day. Continue with the development of your notes. Review the supporting materials in relation to the key ideas you want to develop. Wednesday evening hour: Review your work as a whole and make rhetorical choices regarding the ideas and supporting materials you will actually use.

Day 5: Thursday. Spend an hour or two outlining the sermon. Avoid being overly detailed, but see that your outline reflects clear direction along with the proper coordination and subordination of ideas. After you have completed the outlining of the body of the sermon and have formulated a conclusion, then prepare your introduction. Write out the introduction and conclusion if you wish.

Day 6: Friday. Early in the day spend an hour or two reviewing and polishing your outline. Later in the day spend a half hour or more speaking from your outline. It is quite alright to mumble through a fifteen-minute sermon in five minutes or so, but it may initially take longer because in the process of delivery you will likely become aware of places where you need a clearer transition or even a change in arrangement.

Day 7: Saturday. Review your complete outline briefly but completely at the beginning and end of the day. Prepare the outline or notes you will actually use on Sunday. By now you have probably logged over fifty hours of preparation . . . forty to forty-eight nocturnal hours and six to twelve daytime. Add to that the work of the Spirit and expect good things to happen.

Day 8: Sunday. Enjoy delivering the fruit of your labor. (But in the evening read the texts for next Sunday. Needn't give it a lot of thought. Just soak it in. Download it.) For readers who might think this focused meditation over the whole week is a fresh, new idea, consult Quintilian's *Institutes of Oratory* (AD 95) where the author observes that meditation "never allows itself to be idle." And as for the preparation of a speech or sermon, meditation "connects together the whole texture of speech."[6]

This preparation extended over the entire week allows the sermon to come to you. Whether awake or sleeping, ideas will come because you have provided them a place to come. Relevant supporting materials will emerge from most everywhere as you go about your daily routine. Moreover, the sermon has now become a part of you. You can now visualize the sermon as a whole, your message to your people.

---

6. Quintilian, *Institutes of Oratory*, bk. 10, ch. 6.1.

The fondest hope of this writer is that as you involve yourself with a thoughtful study of sermon preparation you will discover for yourself what the ancients knew so well: Attention to the five rhetorical elements are the means to effective communication. Moreover, you may find that the statement of those five rhetorical elements is a useful sequential description of the process of speech preparation, from the initial task of finding substance for your sermon to the final task of delivering the sermon to your congregation.

The remainder of this text will deal with those five rhetorical elements: Invention, Arrangement, Style, Memory, and Delivery, the elements which give effectiveness to written or oral discourse. The application of those rhetorical elements to your sermon preparation will be based on both classical and contemporary theories of communication.

CHAPTER 1

Invention:
The Search for Content

The Word of God has a thundering authority of its own . . . I've got to preach in such a way that the messages of the text are disclosed in episode, parable, miracle story . . .

—Joseph Sittler, *Gravity and Grace*

The Rhetorical Foundation

JUST AS THE ARCHITECT's plan is developed against a background knowledge of space and materials, the builder of sermons builds most effectively against a background of rhetorical knowledge, the knowledge which helps the speaker find the most effective content, the knowledge which leads to the best arrangement of that content, knowledge which directs the speaker to correct, appropriate, and distinctive language usage, and knowledge which prepares the speaker to deliver the speech/sermon in a manner which is most natural and comfortable for the speaker and also communicates/ connects effectively and directly with the listener.

So, what is this knowledge? What is rhetoric? Rhetoric is the art of giving effectiveness to discourse and may be said to have emerged from the Plato-Gorgias controversy in fourth-century BC Athens. Plato, the philosopher in search of truth, viewed Gorgias and other sophists with skepticism as their careful attention to word usage and their clever use of figures of speech could seem to make the weaker seem to be the stronger case. Plato argued that the orator could not speak effectively, either for teaching or persuasion, until he "knows the truth." In the Phaedrus dialogue Plato has Socrates say: "The first rule of good speaking is to know and speak the truth."[1]

Aristotle's resolution of the controversy observed that in this world we most usually need to act before the truth is ours to know. We act on probabilities based on the best information available. Accordingly, Aristotle defined rhetoric as the art of discovering in any given case the best available means of persuasion.[2] As moderns we might broaden the definition with the term *communication* rather than persuasion and simply view rhetoric as the art of giving effectiveness to discourse. While this text will treat the sermon as a special, even unique genre, it will nevertheless look to basic rhetorical principals as the means to achieve effectiveness in this genre or any other.

A theoretical basis for effective oral and written discourse was established in the fourth century BC with the writing of Aristotle's *Rhetoric*. At that time Athens was the center of world culture, a place where enlightened discourse thrived, both in the political arena and as philosophical debate and dialogue. In that setting Aristotle was the skilled observer capable of making useful generalizations from his observations of such skilled orators as Demosthenes, Aescines, and others. Aristotle's approach to the development of rhetorical theory suggests a basic idea in the Greek conception of art: Since every art follows a method to achieve its end, the method can be analyzed and useful generalizations can be formulated and stated as principles.

Over the years rhetoricians refined and added to the theoretical basis for communication. Quintilian's monumental *Institutes of Oratory* (AD 75) divided the study of rhetoric into five parts, each part a step in the process of speechmaking. Those five are: Invention, Arrangement, Style, Memory, and Delivery. The remainder of

1. Plato, *Phaedrus*.
2. Aristotle, *Rhetoric*, 24.

this chapter will deal with invention, the first part of rhetoric, and will apply basic principles of invention to the process of building a sermon.

Invention

What is the meaning of the term invention?

While the two basic methods of rhetorical invention are fundamentally different, the commonality they share is that both are concerned with finding or discovering content for the speech. In modern terms the task includes both the task of finding ideas and finding ways to develop the ideas. The process of invention is a search, a search for things to say in a speech . . . a search for the substance of your sermon.

The Modes of Invention

The modern speaker ought to take into consideration both the ancient and the modern theories of rhetoric. This is especially true in the case of invention. In the ancient world there were two main methods of invention, one based on form and the other on the subject matter. The formal method was usually divided into two parts, so the ancient rhetoricians actually discussed three separate modes for finding content for the speech. Those theories of invention can be described as follows: Invention based on formal general patterns of the type discussed by Aristotle and later by Cicero, the Roman orator/rhetorician.

This formal pattern identified *topoi* or *loci*, i.e., topics or places that suggest content. For example, useful ideas may be suggested by thinking of your subject in relation to such formal *topoi* or topics as: Contrast, Definition, Description, Significance, Similarities and Differences.

The second pattern for seeking content used the formal parts of a speech, to identify material appropriate to each designated part. For example, John Dewey's analysis of the reflective thinking process has often been applied to speechmaking, so what we might call Dewey's *topoi* for rational analysis would be: Awareness of a problem, definition and clarification of the problem, the solution to the problem, analysis and evaluation.

Applied to sermon preparation, the reflective thinking process described by Dewey suggest these steps for sermon preparation: (1) "Awareness of the problem" becomes awareness of the text, its particular significance and/or its difficulties. (2) "Definition and clarification becomes a placing of the text in context, considering its relation to other texts, and possibly just as important, to other sermons. (3) The "solution" becomes the application of the text to the lives of the listeners, demonstrating how the ancient Word is the contemporary Word, providing fresh insights and perspective in the lives of the listeners.

A concept that differs only slightly from Dewey's reflective thinking process is the idea that every speech occasion can be viewed as a response to a question. Indeed, on the first page of Kenneth Burke's now classic contribution to communication theory, *The Philosophy of Literary Form*, he observes that all "critical and imaginative works are answers to questions posed by the situation in which they arise."[3] Applied to the sermon, the questionnaire analysis then functions as *topoi* in this way: What does the Word say/mean? In what context? To whom addressed? How is the Word related to other texts? How does the Word relate to us, here and now?

Joseph Ratzinger, Pope Benedict XVI, was actually proposing a natural *topoi* for sermons as he suggested a simple three-step question model for sermons or homilies: What are the Scriptures saying? What are the Scriptures saying to me, personally? What should I say to the community in light of its concrete situation?[4]

The third mode of invention is the non-rhetorical view which is based on subject matter, or on a knowledge of the facts. Among the ancient theorists, Plato may be considered the chief advocate for this theory, but every rhetorician since Aristotle has at least

3. Burke, *Philosophy of Literary Form*, 1.
4. Pope Benedict, *Verbum Domini*, 59.

acknowledged this non-rhetorical method. This is the method of the man on the street who says, "If I know my subject, I will know what to say."

So, if one is methodical about the search for content, those are the three methods traditionally described. A bit further on we will look at specific *topoi* relevant to the sermon.

Writings on the subject of invention usually focus on the result of the process . . . the identification of material such as arguments, examples, illustrations, and factual data which serve as supporting materials. To view rhetorical invention adequately one needs to focus on the process itself. What is the process for identifying and selecting appropriate content?

The first step in the process of invention is to determine the purpose of the speech. While the focus of classical rhetoric is on persuasive discourse, contemporary rhetorical theory broadens the description to four kinds of speeches, based on their purpose:

1. To persuade (move to action).
2. To convince (establish belief).
3. To stimulate (a rational or emotional response).
4. To inform.

The sermon might well embrace each of these ends. Indeed, to persuade to action one must first inform, stimulate, and convince. The preacher must have a clear focus on what the sermon is intended to accomplish. A clear sense of purpose provides the needed focus to the search for supporting materials and to the final choice of which supporting materials to use.

The Proofs

The preacher's purpose, what he/she wants the sermon to do (i.e., *active* verb), should be reduced to a single statement. For example, the purpose of Paul's address at the Areopagus might be stated as: To move the audience to abandon idols, repent, and accept the one true God. With a clear purpose in mind, the pastor is half way to the goal of building an effective sermon. The other half involves the proofs. As our old friend Aristotle put it, "There are two parts to a speech. You make a statement and you prove it."

There are three kinds of proof, depending on the nature of the appeal. Logical proof appeals to our rationality. The non-logical appeal is to our emotions, to our human needs. Because an appeal to our rationality is basic, the foundation for all human discourse, the treatment of proofs traditionally begins with the study of logical proof. Indeed, one large church in Monterey, California, advertises, "Sermons for thoughtful and thinking people." While the pastor, no less than the attorney, should be well grounded in the understanding of reasoned discourse, the treatment of proofs here will begin with the non-logical appeals—the ethical and pathetic appeals—because they are the appeals most directly relevant to the sermon.

Pathetic Proof

While rhetorical theorists have provided a significant body of work about logical proof, no such body of information is available for the pathetic and ethical appeals. A reason for this circumstance is that the logical proofs deal directly with the substance of the speech, so useful generalizations can be made both about the substance of logical proof and about the form in which it appears. Pathetic and ethical proofs deal with the adaptation of discourse to a particular audience or person. Human motivation is the substance of non-logical proof and there is no special form in which pathetic and ethical proofs appear. Plato advised the speaker to "know the souls of men."[5] In short, know people and what motivates them. There is no easy course to that knowledge. Nevertheless, the student of speech will do well to study man with as much objectivity as one's methods permit and the subject allows. Indeed, Plato's advice may be particularly relevant to the preacher whose ultimate appeal is

5. Plato, *Phaedrus.*

based on who he/she is and how effective is the outreach of the preacher as a person to all those who sit in the pews.

Words from a dear friend's letter gives concreteness to the importance of the pastor's sensitivity to the human condition, and the need to rightly apply the Word, the freeing gospel message, to today's often harried, stressed-out listener. These words were written at a time when the writer's life was in turmoil: "You will be interested to know that the sermon at church last Sunday (in the midst of all my inner turmoil) was a book report. I guess I just can't relate. I do believe the 'Church is Dead' or dying if somehow we can't make a religion appeal to those of us who have to survive this life too. Someday I hope to meet a preacher who knows that eternity is now and not all them 'streets of gold' later on."[6]

Little did my friend know that Marty Haugen, the gifted contemporary composer, expressed the same thought in his beautifully insightful hymn "Gather Us In":

> Not in the dark buildings confining,
> not in some heaven, light years away-
> here in this place the new light is shining,
> now is the Kingdom, and now is the day.[7]

More recently we hear the same voice from a distant source when Bishop Lino Wanok of Nebbi, Uganda, included in an address to his General Congregation Assembly this observation: "The faithful are longing for preachers . . . who would present the Word of God to them as the voice of Christ speaking to them and to their life situation."[8]

Pathetic proof appeals to the audience's feelings—to their needs, drives, hopes, fears, beliefs, and values. It is unlikely that the preacher will move the listener to belief, conviction, or action without an effective appeal to the listener's feelings and emotions. Accordingly, effective speakers invest a good deal of time in audience analysis. Kenneth Burke, a contemporary theorist, describes

---

6. Bob Mahan, in a personal correspondance with the author, April 1966.

7. Quoted from *Evangelical Lutheran Worship*, 532.

8. Wanok, address to General Congregation Assembly, October 15, 2012.

the process of communication in terms of the speaker's *identification* with the audience's hopes, beliefs, and values. One book on preaching, Craig Loscalzo's *Preaching Sermons That Connect*, carries the subtitle *Effective Communication through Identification*. Indeed, his entire treatise is an application of Burke's concept of identification, or finding common ground that makes real connections with the listener.

Long before Burke's theorizing, the Apostle Paul, in a letter to the church at Corinth, indicates his awareness of the need to identify with his audience, as he writes: "To the Jews, I became a Jew . . . to the weak, I became weak. I have become all things to all people" (1 Cor 9:20).

Paul's speech at the Areopagus is a clear example of audience analysis and the speaker's effort to identify with that audience.

> So Paul, standing in the middle of Areopagus, said: "Men of Athens, I perceive that you are in every way very religious. For as I passed along and observed the objects of your worship, I found also an altar with this inscription, 'To an unknown God.' What therefore you worship as unknown, this I proclaim to you. The God who made the world and everything in it, being Lord of heaven and earth, does not live in shrines made by man, nor is he served by human hands, as though he needed anything, since he himself gives to all men life and breath and everything. And he made from one every nation of men to live on all the face of the earth, having determined allotted periods and the boundaries of their habitation that they should seek God in the hope that they might feel after him and find him. Yet he is not far from each one of us, for in him we live and move and have our being, even as some of your poets have said, 'For we are indeed his offspring.'" (Acts 17:22–28)

In sum, pathetic proof is far more than a stirring of the emotions. Effective pathetic appeal comes from a right understanding of the human condition. It identifies and appeals to the needs, wants, hopes, fears, beliefs, and values which motivate people to belief and action.

Ethical Proof

Ethos, ethical proof, the appeal generated by the speaker as a person may be the least understood means of support. In biblical terms, it is the good shepherd who knows his flock. Theorists since Aristotle have agreed that the factors of ethical proof are the speaker's reputation for good sense, good will, and good moral character. A speaker's *ethos* is the *power to motivate the listener to accept the speaker's beliefs and judgments because the listener accepts the speaker as a person.* St. Augustine put it this way: "The life of the speaker has greater weight in determining whether he is obediently heard than any grandness of eloquence."[9]

How important is ethical proof? For any speaker, it may be the most important appeal. For the pastor, it is almost certainly most important. Indeed, the pastor's ethos is built from the pastor's many roles: teacher, counselor, evangelist, advocate, witness, high priest, and servant. The person who preaches the sermon, who raises up the gospel message, must reflect the elements of ethical proof well beyond the standard applied to others. For certain, the gospel message of love and compassion, as reflected in the life and language of the pastor, is an overwhelmingly powerful ethical proof . . . the ultimate in walking the walk and talking the talk.

An astonishing illustration of ethical proof, the power of the person, is found in Raul Castro's 2015 meeting with Pope Francis. From the personal contact and from reading the pope's sermons and speeches, the communist Castro was so impressed by Francis's good sense, good will, and moral character that he declared his intention to return to the practice of prayer and worship.

In addition to the ethical appeal brought to the pulpit because of who the pastor is known to be, the sermon itself may add or detract from the ethical appeal. For example, excellence in the use of reasoned discourse and in clear arrangement communicates good sense. The insightful use of pathetic appeal together with sincerity expressed in the delivery suggests good character and good will. In the words of George Campbell, author of *Pulpit Eloquence* (1824),

9. Augustine, *De doctrina christiana*, 4.26.56.

the sermon is "not just of ideas only, but of sentiments, passions, dispositions, and purposes."[10]

The speaker who can most effectively employ ethical proof is the speaker who has earned a reputation for being a person of good will, good judgment, and good character and whose speech adds further evidence for the good reputation he or she enjoys. The preacher is a person speaking.

Logical Proof

Consistent with Aristotle's definition of rhetoric, classical rhetoric focused on persuasion, with extensive attention to logical proof. While much of contemporary public speaking has or should have its basis in *logos*, the appeal based on sound arguments and clear reasoning, preaching may be regarded as unique, a genre that proclaims the truth. Look for example, to the opening words of Pastor Muester's Easter sermon. The proclamation is made: "The Lord is Risen! He is Risen Indeed!" While the starting point of his sermon, or yours, may be the gospel truth, the pastor nevertheless carries the obligation of every advocate . . . to make the truth seem to be true.

While logical proof is not likely to be a primary means of support in the development of your sermon, it is nevertheless important that the pastor be knowledgeable regarding this aspect of rhetoric, the anatomy of reasoned discourse, a guide to the thinking process.

The pastor needs to relate the Word to the world, a world filled with contentious issues, a rhetorical world with few certainties, many probabilities. The educated person, certainly the pastor, needs the tools to navigate these uncertain waters, tools to enhance one's rational discourse and to recognize and deal with irrational discourse. Logical proof is the currency of rational thinking and of reasoned discourse.

10. Campbell, *Lectures on Pulpit Eloquence.*

Reasoned discourse is called argument. Attempts to describe argument range from the simple "if P then Q" to complex descriptions such as Stephen Toulman's structural analysis. Whatever description is used, the key word in the analysis of argument is *relationship*, the relationship of the premises to the conclusion. Every argument infers a conclusion from premises.

To say that Bill is a naughty boy is a statement of opinion, possibly a statement of fact, and possibly a premise, but it is not an argument because no inference is made. To say that Bill is a naughty boy, *therefore* he is going to get into trouble is an argument. If P then Q. It is the *inference* that makes it an argument. That is, accepted facts or assertions (evidence) are related in such a way that a previously unrecognized fact or assertion (conclusion) becomes evident. Useful arguments are most readily invented when the speaker knows well both the substance of the subject and the form in which reasoned discourse appears. Forming, finding, or analyzing an argument, then, is about an awareness of relationships, how facts or circumstances relate to one another. (Discovering new relationships is the essence of creativity.) Forming and finding arguments centers on an awareness of relationships, how facts or circumstances relate to one another. A challenge to every preacher is to discover new relationships in the Word, new applications of the Word.

In order to cognitively deal with the process of inference, we need to describe what we are talking about. Arguments may be described either by their form, the shape they take, or by their substance, the functional relationship of the evidence to the conclusion. In describing arguments according to their form, the arguments may be stated categorically, hypothetically, or disjunctively. These three forms may be seen in the following examples of statement and proof:

The church should sell the aging parsonage:

1. The current economic situation renders ownership uneconomical.

    (Categorical)

2. If the parsonage is not sold, the church will
continue to deplete its cash reserves.

(Hypothetical)

3. Either we sell the parsonage now or we
could face foreclosure within two years.

(Disjunctive)

While the form of argument is important, it only describes
how the argument is stated. More important is the substance of the
argument, *how* the evidence is related to the conclusion. In general, the evidence will be related in one of two ways: Evidence will
function to assert *that* the conclusion is warranted, or the evidence
will function to assert *why* the conclusion is warranted.

While there are many ways to describe arguments, none are
clearer, more concise, or more useful than that of Richard Whately, a nineteenth-century English pastor, prelate, and logician who
described four kinds of argument. The first three, argument from
sign, example, and analogy serve the function of indicating *why*
the conclusion follows from the premises. Any description of argument ought to indicate the relationship of the evidence to the
conclusion. The relationship may be described as follows:

1. Argument from Sign: The sign relationship asserts that the
presence of A (evidence) is an indication of the presence of
B (conclusion). For example: It's 11:00 p.m. and the lights are
still on in the church office (sign). It looks like the pastor is
working overtime (conclusion).

2. Argument from Example: The relationship is from specific
instances to a general conclusion. The argument asserts that a
generalization is warranted if based on enough relevant, specific instances. The specific instances function as evidence to
support the generalization. For example Pastors A, B, C, and
D from Gettysburg Seminary are all excellent preachers, so
Gettysburg must be doing a good job in homiletics instruction. It should be observed that argument from example is
basic to every other argument, for every other argument is

based on a generalization, which is either stated or implied. It is the argument from example that makes these generalizations. Accordingly, as you analyze reasoned discourse (argument), *always look for the generalization on which the argument is based.*

3. Argument from Analogy: The relationship of the evidence to the conclusion is from particular instances to at least one other instance. The argument asserts that if facts (evidence) relating to B are alike in some essential respects, they will be alike in at least one other respect. For example: The pastor's involvement with X, Y, and Z show her unselfish work habits, but may be unproductive in the long run, just as it was for me in graduate school when I . . .

4. Argument from Cause: The relationship is from cause to effect. The argument asserts that if event A exists it will cause event B to follow. Or, in the case of past fact, the reasoning is that if event B was followed by A, then A is the cause of B. For example, if the pastor continues to work day and night, she will not have time for her family.

In summary, the speaker who knows the forms of argument may then use them as *topoi*. As form is related to substance, the speaker can proceed as one who knows the anatomy of argument, so can effectively analyze, take apart, the reasoned discourse of others and more effectively utilize reasoned discourse where appropriate.

Notes on Invention as Applied to the Sermon

My own church has produced a useful definition of the sermon in its publication *The Use of the Means of Grace: A Statement on the Practice of Word and Sacrament*: "Preaching is the living and contemporary voice of one who interprets in all the Scriptures the things concerning Jesus Christ. In fidelity to the readings appointed for the day, the preacher proclaims our need of God's grace and freely offers that grace, equipping the community for mission and service in daily life."[11]

If accepted as adequate,* the definition provides clear direction for both the purpose and general content for preaching. The sermon, it says:

1. Will be based on the lectionary text.

2. Will interpret; explicate the word for the day.

3. Will proclaim the need for grace, and will offer that grace.

4. Will apply the gospel text to the congregation to encourage and prepare them to act out their faith in this world. As Carl Barth observed, the preacher should have both Bible and newspaper in hand.

If one were to add to this list it would be that the sermon will apply the Word to offer hope and healing to the many listeners likely to be in need of both.

The need to apply the gospel text to the congregation is stated so clearly and well in *The Grace-full Use of the Means of Grace*: "The sermon is always bridgework, linking the eternal and gracious counsel of God to the life of this particular assembly of believers. Thus, even as the sermon proclaims God's everlasting mercy as the light for the world, it does so in such a way as to shed that light upon the world, illuminating for the assembly of believers the circumstances in which they presently live. And from that proclamation the assembly will be dismissed into the world for witness and service and acts of justice and mercy."[12]

In sum, the gospel is read, explained, and applied. In addition to the inventive process appropriate for all discourse, consider these suggestions particular to the sermon:

1. Appreciate and trust in the truth, power, and authority of the Word, but do not assume its authority.

---

11. *Use of the Means of Grace*, 9.
* See appendix B for a disclaimer.
12. *Grace-full Use of the Means of Grace*, 7.

That is, the truth needs to be made to seem true, and that is the pastor's job, the central task of the sermon. In Joseph Sittler's words, "For most people, 'what the Bible says' is no more authoritative than what the *New York Times* or *Washington Post* says."[13]

Sittler explains in a manner which shines a bright light on the essential nature of building a sermon: "The authority of Scripture has to depend on the text's internal congruity with the human pathos . . . the reality of what it means to be a human being in this appalling time. . . . And that Word will be invested with authority by virtue of its liberating, enlightening, and promising congruity, not by virtue of 'the Bible says.'"[14]

In short, the sermon, the Word, can make sense to the listener, can *connect* with the person in the pew, because when the preacher applies the Word to the circumstances of the real world, the Word really does make sense.

2. Place the Word for the day in context.

The focus on only the lectionary text without regard to the context may be inadequate or even misleading to the interpretation. What comes before the designated text? What follows? Even if not essential to the full meaning of the text, the companion verses often provide relevant material of interest, information which helps build the congregation's Bible literacy. See, for example, Pastor John Rollefson's sermon in the appendix for the effective use of appropriate, relevant scripture apart from the lectionary text.

3. Build an introduction which serves as a bridge from the gospel reading to the sermon content.

More will be said on this in the next chapter's discussion of arrangement, but it needs to be shouted from the hilltop that the preacher can, and preachers do, completely derail the train of thought from gospel text to sermon by not using the introduction, the opening moments, to create a bridge from the gospel text to the sermon content.

13. Sittler, *Gravity and Grace*, 47.
14. Ibid.

4. Relate the text for the day to similar concepts stated so well in the church's hymns and liturgies.

The word in song is often a powerful poetic statement of the Word for the day. Many texts, for example, can be related to the grace-filled hymn "Joyful, Joyful, We Adore Thee." The genius of Beethoven and Van Dyke are there to enrich your own creativity and there is a treasure trove in every church which can provide meaning with which the listener can easily identify. Certain texts may direct the pastor to a specific hymn. For example, 1 John 3:1 says, "Behold what manner of love the Father has bestowed on us, that we should be called children of God." The concept *children of God* can so easily and wonderfully be related to the hymn "Children of the Heavenly Father." Finding such relationships often serves as an excellent introduction, as is illustrated below.

In the introduction to an ordination sermon titled "Commitment," Donald McLeod, founder and first president of the Academy of Homiletics, relates the text of John 17:19, "For their sakes I consecrate myself that they also might be consecrated by the truth," to a familiar hymn:

> Take my hands, and let them move
> At the impulse of thy love.
> Take my feet, and let them be
> Swift and beautiful for thee . . .
> Take my-self, and I will be
> Ever only, all for thee.[15]

Pastor McLeod introduced that hymn after reporting on Billy Graham's visit to Harvard University where he asked the university president, Dr. Bok, "What in your opinion is the greatest lack in the mind-set of students today?" And Dr. Bok replied, "A sense of commitment."[16]

Pastor McLeod then relates the message of the hymn to the message of the Word from John as he asks: "I wonder how many of

15. Cox, *Best Sermons*, 147.
16. Ibid.

us pause to realize the risk we are assuming . . . [as] verse by verse we offer some one of our capacities or powers to God's exclusive use."

The same opportunity for enrichment can be found in a church's liturgical statements, whether ancient or contemporary. The language found in Marty Haugen's "Hymn of Morning Praise," for example, a part of his *Service of Light*, has enough beauty and power to inspire or enrich many sermons. Feel these words: "Let your light scatter the darkness and shine within your people here. . . . God of daybreak, God of shadows, come and light our hearts anew."[17]

Or take a very close look at the words of the often-used liturgical song/prayer "Create in Me." What is the meaning of each of those six supplications? State each one as a question. Is there not inspiration enough in each line for a whole sermon?

> Create in me a clean heart, O God,
> and renew a right spirit within me.
> Cast me not away from your presence
> and take not your Holy Spirit from me.
> Restore unto me the joy of your salvation,
> and uphold me with your spirit free.

With regard to identification, the use of liturgical material can relate the text to what is already familiar to the listener and provide an appeal of special significance as it relates *what God says to us* in the gospel with what *we say to God* in the liturgy. (Appendix D illustrates this *we speak/God speak* dialogue in an application to stewardship.)

People come to worship to encounter God, to feel a holy presence in the reading of the Word, the singing of the Word in hymns, the Word in liturgy, and the Word in the sermon. The preacher who relates all those elements in the sermon creates an integrated worship service, an organic whole.

17. Haugen, *Service of Light*, 2, 3.

5. In a similar vein, relate the text for the day to the hymns, liturgy, and creeds specifically to clarify the nature of *worship as dialogue.*

The substance of every worship service may be viewed as dialogue: what the Lord speaks to us in the Word and what we speak to the Lord in our hymns, liturgies, and creeds. There is an intimate connection between thought and speech, but if we speak the same words often enough, the connection may become lost, so words are spoken with little or no thought. Owing to the human condition, which allows for speech without thought, it may be a good thing from time to time to renew the vitality of this dialogue by devoting a service to the *meaning* of what we say to the Lord.

Such a focus on meaning can enrich a sermon. But also, an entire sermon could focus on worship as dialogue, relating what is said by the people to what is said by the Lord. Both the Word of the Lord and the hymns and liturgies have meaning relevant to current issues of concern to the church and its people.

6. Refer the text for the day to other texts similar in content, or to other texts which relate in a way that provides further insight.

For example, the concepts so beautifully stated in the Twenty-Third Psalm can be augmented and illuminated by the detailed description of the gatekeeper included in John 10:1–15. Billy Graham did this extensively, in a way which illuminated both his sermons and the listener's grasp of the Bible. So, as a part of your inventive process, get in the habit of using a concordance to identify useful texts which can help clarify meaning, expand and enrich the text for the day, and function to introduce your congregation to the Bible as a whole.

7. Relate the text to a previous sermon and/or to a future one.

In addition to the positive teaching moment vis-à-vis biblical awareness, you undergird the message of a previous sermon and contribute to the unity and coherence of the overall worship experience. As you relate the text to a future sermon you create expectations. To create and fulfill expectations, whether within a single sermon or with regard to a future sermon is an especially effective means of communication.

8. Use the beauty and power of metaphor creatively.

A sermon given several years ago by Bishop Chris Boerger on the Lazarus resurrection story in John is still clearly remembered because it was both creative and compelling as it employed three metaphoric applications: The stone to be rolled away was whatever keeps us from acting out our faith. The stench was the wickedness in the world. The admonition "Unbind him. Let him go" became an admonition to the listener to free themselves from whatever restrains them from faithful service.

9. Avoid willful content.

Having just heard a terrific story or having been charmed by a novel illustration is inadequate reason to somehow work it into your sermon if it does not fit. These cute, sometimes humorous asides almost always function to create visual images in the mind which may occupy the listener's attention well beyond the telling of the story, and so function to detract from the sermon's real substance.

10. Do not avoid controversial issues in the manner of the pussyfooter, but utilize the Word to address the issue.

As a citizen of both the kingdom and the public realm, the preacher is understandably sensitive to divisive issues in the public sphere. In such cases, it may be best, and it may be adequate, to let the Word speak for itself. But it is the pastor who must find the Word that speaks to the issues. The Word speaks often and eloquently to the issues of poverty, violence, and injustice, but it is the pastor who applies the gospel of grace, peace, and love to the contemporary scene. That treasure has been placed in earthen vessels. As an example of applying God's word to a burning issue of the day, reference is again made to John Rollefson's sermon on the encounter of Philip with the eunuch, which you will find in appendix A.

In an Easter sunrise service in 1968, when the burning issue was the legitimacy of the Vietnam War, the Word spoke subtly but clearly by using this contrasting language to address the issue: "The message of Easter is a proclamation of redemptive love. . . . In a word, the message of Easter is *Life*. The good word of Easter contrasts with . . . death and violence, searching and destroying."[18]

In his sermon on 1 Corinthians 12:9, Dietrich Bonhoeffer speaks to all Christians as he pleads for Christian courage against the backdrop of Nazi power. Although preached in another time, Bonhoeffer leaves us a statement to be pondered by all who preach, and a statement certain to bring a smile to the present Pope Francis. Bonhoeffer declared:

> Christianity stands or falls with its revolutionary protest against violence, arbitrariness and pride of power and with its plea for the weak. Christians are doing too little to make these points clear rather than too much. Christendom adjusts itself far too easily to the worship of power. Christians should give more offense, shock the world far more than they are doing now. Christians should take a stronger stand in favor of the weak rather than considering first the possible right of the strong.[19]

A similar message is given to a new generation as Martin Luther King, writing from the Birmingham jail, speaks of the contemporary church's voice as often weak and ineffectual, with an uncertain sound.

Can the church make a difference in public affairs? In politics? It certainly seemed so to Bono, the celebrity rock music singer who spoke to congressional leaders and to President George W. Bush at a Prayer Breakfast in Washington, DC. Bono described the church's potential for influence as he observed: "When churches started demonstrating on debt, governments listened—and acted. When churches started organizing, petitioning, and even that

18. Lay preacher, Easter sunrise service, Richland, Washington, 1968.
19. Bonhoeffer, Sermon on 2 Cor. 12:19.

most unholy of acts today, God forbid, *lobbying* on AIDS and global health, governments listened—and acted. I'm here today in all humility to say: you changed minds; you changed policy; and you changed the world."[20]

The church's stand in reference to the weak and the poor, and the Scripture's direction regarding violence and injustice is clear, unambiguous whether in Bonhoeffer's time or ours. It is not so clear whether enough is being said from the pulpit to address these issues. Civil issues should inform the pulpit and the pulpit should inform civil issues.

Today's most divisive issues center on changes in societal norms. To remember that each generation experiences such changes comes as cool comfort for those of us who find ourselves as shocked and puzzled with today's social scene as the disciples were when they found Jesus at the Samaritan well.

In a *New York Times* Op-Ed piece titled "The Next Culture War," David Brooks addresses the decline of Christianity and church attendance in the United States. Brooks observes that the cultural norms Christians have long held sacred no longer exist, that much of the divisiveness centers in the sexual revolution, and that the church's response has had a negative effect on more than one generation. The church has allowed its attention to changing values to detract from the richness of the faith it professes. Brooks advises the church not to be distracted, to put aside that culture war.

But do not put aside your trust in the unchanging, life-changing, life-affirming power and authority of the Word. In a time of unprecedented, rapid change, not only in societal mores, but in technology and in world economics and politics, *people seek solid ground*.

Wherever the meaning "fundamentalist preacher" is actually the preacher who is focused on the fundamentals of the Word, on the basic New Testament truths of love, joy, peace, patience, kindness, generosity, faithfulness, gentleness, and self-control, the

---

20. Bono, keynote address, 54th National Prayer Breakfast.

people will find solid ground. The people will discover from the pulpit a bridge over troubled waters, a solid unchanging rock.

11. Help your congregation to see the Bible as a whole, the relationship of its parts, and its unifying central themes.

You can go a long way toward doing this by setting aside a half day to review the lectionary texts for at least a period of four to six weeks in advance. Note such things as common themes, unusual relationships, and even apparent contradictions. Some of the "future texts" will enrich your current sermon. Others will present opportunities to create expectations. Just as Joshua set up twelve stones in Gilgal to stimulate curiosity among the children, the preacher can create curiosity and create expectations with a thoughtful reference to a future text. For example, "Next week we will hear Paul address the Romans on this same subject, but you will hear him reaffirming these principles to a different audience in quite a different manner." Create curiosity. Create interest in the Word. Create expectations. Then fulfill those expectations.

12. Take time for reflection.

Joseph Sittler has observed that "the principal work of the ordained ministry is reflection: cultivation of one's penetration into the depth of the Word so that the witness may be poignant and strong."[21] Although the busy pastor might find this advice a hard sell with his church council, the intention is pure gold. The pastor does need leisure time and the discipline to use it wisely. The well can go dry. And it is the dry well that results in what Joseph Sittler describes as "sermons rich in piety and oversimplification."[22]

Even the good soil needs nourishment. When the crowds were pressing for the apostle's attention, Jesus advised them to "come away to a deserted place all by yourselves and rest awhile." Even Christ's ministry required periods of solitude. Indeed, Henri Nouwen reminds us that after an extraordinarily busy day Christ followed it with a period of solitude: "In the morning, long before

21. Sittler, *Gravity and Grace*, 49.
22. Ibid., 50.

dawn, he got up and left the house and went off to a lonely place and prayed there."[23]

Bonhoeffer has observed that the early morning belongs to the church of the risen Christ . . . early morning, a time for the kind of reflection on the Word suggested in the schedule for sermon preparation described in the introduction. Good sermons require reflection. Reflection requires solitude.

Making the Content Interesting

Attention determines response. Audience attention is given to interesting content. So, after the pastor has identified appropriate content for the sermon, how is that content made interesting enough to hold the listener's attention?

Two keys to an interest building, interest holding speech of any kind is to have *variety and concreteness*. Good speeches almost always exhibit a good deal of variety in both form and substance. The form may vary from description to argument, from anecdote to example, from dialogue to comparison. The speaker should think about variety in the preparation process and experiment with different forms.

The substance may include examples, illustrations, narrative, description, statistics, definitions, questions, and quotations. While the possibilities for building variation into the sermon are great, the principle is simply that variety should be present. A lack of variety has its effect on both the listener and the speaker. The listener loses attention; the speaker loses those triggers which stimulate interesting delivery as the sameness in the content leads to a sameness in voice, possibly even resulting in a monotone.

A further means to enhance the speaker's ability to get and maintain attention is concreteness. Specific, concrete materials are far more likely to be given attention than generalized statements.

To build and hold interest, include content which is familiar to the listener as well as that which is novel. Use the compelling

23. Nouwen, *Out of Solitude*, 5.

nature of suspense as well as conflict and consider that which is tragic as well as that which is comical. In sum, make your sermon interesting by making it appealing in a variety of ways. If you wish to dip your toe in the well of sound teaching by example, read chapter 7 of Barbara Brown Taylor's *An Altar in the World*. Illustrations range from Buddhist teachings to the ruminations of a first-year seminary student. Examples range from a Swedish film to a fire escape used as sanctuary. Such varied, relevant, concrete imagery also makes her sermons interesting and compelling. Yours too.

The following material discusses the variety of forms employed in all discourse. The effective speaker or writer uses them skillfully to communicate meaning and to provide variety.

Definition. Any enumeration of supporting material is likely to give definition a principal place, and this is all the more so as the pastor delves into the text. Definition, often the key to understanding, is frequently employed in the beginning of a speech to clarify just what the subject is and perhaps to limit the scope of the subject. Any definition the speaker employs should have meaning for the particular audience and should be precise enough to avoid either vagueness or ambiguity.

Many biblical names and terms require definition. Even reasonably common terms such as Sadducees and Pharisees or sanctification and grace will benefit from definition and explanation. Strange place names such as Kadesh or Jappa need to be identified, and in doing so the pastor enriches the sermon with potentially interesting, novel material. In the same way, ancient monetary terms such as talent or shekel are given meaning through definition. The parable of the Talents, for example, has much greater meaning if the value of the talent is known.

Examples. The speaker may communicate meaning by citing specific instances, called examples because they serve to exemplify . . . to illustrate and clarify the speaker's meaning. Effective examples give clarity and concreteness to the sermon, and these are two important characteristics of discourse which builds interest and sustains it. The pastor, for example, may give concrete meaning to the broad term "good neighbor" by examples ranging from the Good Samaritan story to the current outreach of the church to the world's hungry and homeless. In choosing which examples to use, the pastor should think beyond the matter of clarification to the possibility of discovering valuable teaching moments relevant to one's own congregation. For example, speaking of the good neighbor, Barbara Brown Taylor observes that the Hebrew Bible includes one verse with the command to love one's neighbor, but in thirty-six places commands us to love the stranger.

Illustrations. An extended example is called an illustration. The illustration may be real or hypothetical. As its name implies, the illustration employs language to draw a mental picture. Illustrations can serve as a highly effective means of development as audiences almost always enjoy and pay attention to a vivid illustration.

Nevertheless, a word of caution is in order regarding their use. Because illustrations provide material which is easily delivered and is often entertaining, speakers sometimes get "carried away" with the illustration. The cardinal rule is that the illustration should be relevant to the point and actually function to clarify or develop the sermon's purpose. The length of the illustration should always be in proportion to the importance of the point being illustrated.

Statistics. Another means of development which lends concreteness to a speech is the employment of statistical data. The speaker who has the figures at hand reveals to the audience that he/she has "done the homework." Statistics are often essential to making the idea clear. For example, the pastor can speak in general terms about hunger and homelessness in the local community, but only by providing specific, factual information on the subject is the pastor likely to get the attention needed to lead to a positive response. For example, in contrast to just hearing general information about poverty in their up-scale community, parishioners are far more likely to respond to specificity such as the fact that 34 percent of the communities children are living below the poverty level.

Two rules and a general caution apply to the use of statistics:

1. Be certain your statistics are accurate. If your figures appear unusual or if they contradict generally accepted information, you should comment on that, and cite your source.

2. Be sure your statistics are meaningful to your audience, especially if the data involves large numbers. You may safely assume that your listener is cognitively unable to conceptualize the meaning of million, billion, and trillion. The speaker may communicate meaning by devising a brief illustration so the listener may visualize the amount. For example, the lowest ten year cost estimate for the invasion of Iraq is $3.8 trillion, an incomprehensible figure until broken down to $1 billion dollars a day, or over $40 million per hour.

Questions. Posing a question is a great way to connect with the listener. Questions get people's attention. People respond to questions because, as Gerhard Frost so aptly observes, we are "God's question asking creatures."[24]

In a sermon preached in Duke University Chapel, the Reverend Sam Wells related Christian faith to the work and passion of the artist, concluding his sermon with a series of questions: "Are you an artist? According to Psalm 150 you are. . . . Are you a prophet, seeking truth and a closer social embodiment of it? Are you a priest, rolling back the veil between heaven and earth? Are you a king, rousing all creation to its potential and praise? Are you allowing the Holy Spirit to make you a work of art that turns all creation into alleluia?"[25]

Quotations and Literary References. An interesting way to develop a thought is to make a reference to the ideas of others by the use of quotations or more extended literary references. The resources available to the speaker are as rich and varied as one's knowledge of the world's history and literature. An estimate of the worth of such materials is indicated by the popularity of books which purport to have quotations for all occasions. While such

---

24. Frost, *It Had Better Be True*, 6.
25. Wells, "Turning All into Alleluia."

books make interesting reading, the best source is the mental storehouse of the well educated person.

John Steinbeck's observation about reading, that to write well we need to read well, can be applied equally to those who wish to speak well. And, as one reads, a useful habit for a pastor is to identify potentially useful materials from one's reading and maintain a subject file for future use.

As a caution in the use of quotations, it should be clear that the speaker must be guided by principles of accuracy and honesty in the use of the statements of others. While direct quotations do not always have to be employed, the speaker must always use good judgment to be as exact as the case requires. The principle of honesty simply means that credit will be given for expressions or ideas which are not one's own.

Analogy. The human mind has a natural propensity for making observations of new phenomena in terms of its likenesses and similarities to what is known. By definition an analogy is a stated or implied likeness between two things which have attributes in common, but are not identical.

The two kinds of analogy are the figurative and the literal. Comparing the kingdom of heaven to a mustard seed is a figurative analogy. The likeness is not in the things themselves, but in characteristics which may be attributed to each.

The literal analogy makes its comparisons within the same class of things, as with a church to a church, or a denomination to a denomination.

Analogies are useful to the speaker because they often liken something new or unknown to something familiar and in that process of identification they may render the listener more open to accept the new because he has already accepted the old. In writing to the believers in Corinth, Paul employed the figurative analogy of the Olympic Games as he compared the Christian life to a race well run. As you know, Christ often spoke in parables, extended analogies which served to teach new truths in an interesting form with which his listeners could easily identify.

The extensive use of explanation by analogy leads to another word of caution. Because analogies are so easily employed, some speakers tend to overuse them and sometimes construct an entire speech on the basis of a bad analogy. Observe in the model sermons how analogy has been used effectively and experiment with this form of development yourself. Fr. Valentine's homily "Finding God at the Heart of Things" illustrates the richness analogy can bring to the content.

Comparison and Contrast. This form of development is actually a form of exposition or analogy, but it proceeds by revealing similarities and differences between two or more things and it almost always makes its comparisons between the same class of things. For example, a person wishing to clarify the differences in eighteenth-century Puritan theology might compare and contrast the divergent theologies of John Calvin and Martin Luther, of God Law and God Love.

Description. Description can be a particularly interesting aspect of discourse, especially if the description is specific and concrete. For example, a sermon on the Twenty-Third Psalm came alive when the preacher, a missionary from Jordan, painted detailed images of the countryside and described accurately and concretely the narrow gate and just how and why the shepherds anoint the head with oil.

Narrative. Everyone loves a good story and narrative is often employed as interesting supporting material which enriches the dialogue. Christ, the preacher, used narrative frequently. Caution suggests that narrative always be relevant, to the point, and not overused. The speaker, even the preacher, can get carried away by a good story. An example of engaging, effective use of narrative is found in the sermon *God Is In This Place*, which you will find in appendix A. Rabbi Alissa Wise uses a personal narrative as an introduction as she ties a text from Genesis to her central theme.

In sum, there is a rich array of material to provide content to support the speaker's main ideas in a manner that will be interesting because it is vivid, specific, and concrete. The cardinal rule is that the speaker build the speech with a variety of the forms of support.

A Note on the Sameness of Sermon and Service

An emphasis on variety is important for any speech. It is of particular importance for the sermon because of the distinctive circumstances in which the sermon is given. Every sermon is at risk because it is given against the background of "the same old." Distinctive? What other speaking occasion presents, week after week, the same setting, the same speaker (usually), the same general subject, and more or less the same audience?

Accordingly, the pastor needs to bring vitality to the sermon, in part with a variety of interest-building, interest-holding, relevant supporting materials and partly through intelligent and creative arrangement which avoids the same organizational pattern in each sermon, and finally through the use of concrete, clear, vivid language along with effective delivery. The organization of the sermon's content, language usage, style, memory, and delivery are the subjects of subsequent chapters, but for now let us address the ubiquitous problem of sameness in the sermon and in the service.

For both the preacher and the listener this sameness can have a numbing influence on the whole worship experience. Pastor and people can find themselves going through the motions, so caught up in the form of the service that the substance is missed. Creative means are needed to retain vitality in the sermon and in the overall worship experience. The following suggestions are offered to emphasize some of what has gone before, and to stimulate your own thinking on the need to bring vitality to the worship experience:

1. Build an integrated worship experience. Vitality in the service depends on giving life to the Word. An effective way to build a worship experience which maximizes attention to the Word and achieves unity and coherence is to embrace the Word in music, liturgy, and scripture. The pitfalls of sameness can be

largely avoided in an organic service with meaningful, related parts.

2. Change the sermon in both form and substance. Achieve both variety and vitality through an amalgamation of the pastor's sermon with congregational Bible study. To do this, for example: The church's newsletter would announce the lectionary texts for the month and the Sunday bulletin would include the texts for the coming week. In effect, the congregation is given opportunity and encouragement to think about the texts all during the week.

Then, in place of the regular sermon, the preacher would make a three to five minute informal presentation on his/her thoughts on the meaning of the text and its application to the listeners. Emphasis here is on informal . . . possibly no notes, certainly no manuscript, sans pulpit. This presentation would then be followed by five to eight minutes where members of the congregation would have the opportunity to make their observations on the text or address questions to the pastor regarding the text. Finally, the pastor would spend three to five minutes summarizing and responding to questions.

This kind of amalgamation might best be initiated in the summertime, on an experimental basis. It might prove to have real benefits for both pastor and congregation. It should be noted too that the inclusion of the lectionary text for the following Sunday is a highly recommended practice, quite apart from whether this "amalgamation" form is used for the sermon. It may be one of the very best means to stimulate congregational Bible study.

3. Achieve variety by changing the length of the sermon. Where is it written that sermons need to be fifteen minutes, or twenty, or any prescribed length? It is your sermon, so it is your call on whether it is to be eight minutes or twenty four. If the sermon is to be unusually long or short, the preacher might comment on that.

4. Achieve variety and vitality by utilizing a varied pattern of arrangement from sermon to sermon. For certain, see that you do not utilize the same pattern of arrangement week after week. In a local church the pattern went unchanged for months: First, an introduction that may or may not be related to the Word for the day. Second, a statement of three parts to be developed. Third, the development. Fourth, a re-statement and brief conclusion. There is nothing wrong with such a structured pattern, but to hear it, or any other pattern, repeated week after week can be deadening, both for the preacher and the listeners, as was the case in the example above. To work with and to hear different patterns is stimulating for both. Consider the different patterns that might be appropriate for the parable of the prodigal son. My choices for that text would be the spacial or chronological, but the most famous sermon I know on that text, Helmut Thielicke's *The Waiting Father*, employed neither. The choice is personal, but almost any choice you make offers intriguing possibilities.

5. Achieve variety in the worship service by occasionally presenting the Word in music, or the word in the liturgy (sans "sermon"). Depending on the human resources in the congregation, the pastor or the minister of music might relate the texts for the day, Word in scripture, to the Word in music. A hymn such as "Joyful, Joyful, We Adore Thee" could perfectly relate to dozens of texts. And a single text could relate beautifully to many hymns.

In the same manner, in a worship service centering on the liturgy, the pastor would relate how *what we say to God* in the liturgy connects with *what God says to us* in the scriptures. Appendix D provides an example of such dialogue and how it can be applied to a particular purpose.

These kinds of worship services, centered on the Word, can serve to illuminate for the congregation the manner in which the means of grace include the Word read, the Word in the hymns sung, and the Word in the liturgy spoken.

6. A different kind of variety can be achieved with occasional pulpit exchanges. There are obvious advantages and disadvantages to such exchanges and to be comfortable with them, both the pastor and the congregation has to view them as advantageous. The same can be said of the potential benefits of the layman's Sunday experience, something that again needs to be viewed positively by both pastor and congregation. If it is a positive experience for the congregation, and depending on the human resources, lay persons might preach more or less often.

Summary

Invention is the process by which the speaker discovers materials and ideas relevant to the subject, to the speaker's purpose, and to the audience. The process of discovery is followed by the process of rhetorical choice, selecting that supporting material which is most relevant, most interesting, most appropriate, and adequate for the purpose.

When the speaker has determined what materials will be used, the next question is: In what order should the materials be presented? The response to that question is the province of *arrangement*, traditionally the second part of the subject of rhetoric and the subject of our attention in the following chapter.

CHAPTER 2

Arrangement of the Content

Order is heaven's first law.

—Alexander Pope, *An Essay on Man*

AMONG THE VIRTUES TO be valued and emulated, orderliness ought to compete with cleanliness as second only to godliness. Orderliness not only helps to keep us sane, but it helps others to make sense of what we are saying. Accordingly, the second canon of classical rhetoric, *dispositio* or arrangement, functions to give orderliness to discourse.

While there are many patterns of organization, all have the same objective—to provide clarity, unity, and direction to the speech. The most common patterns are the logical, chronological, spacial, psychological, and topical. Before looking at these, it should be noted that *any* pattern of arrangement can also function as *topoi* for invention, *as the pattern itself suggests substance to fill the particular form.*

Standard Patterns of Organization

Through the process of arrangement the speaker gives order to the materials of the speech. The result should be a sermon with purposeful form which is coherent and unified and has a clear sense of direction. These qualities of orderliness make the sermon both easier to deliver and easier to follow as a listener:

1. The Logical Pattern: The principle that applies here is that the materials are arranged according to the continuity of the reasoning process. Logical analysis takes the subject apart, identifies the parts, then distributes the parts appropriately for the clearest development of the subject.

A logical pattern may follow a deductive or inductive method. The deductive method may state the scriptural topic together with the main heads under which it is to be developed. For example, the pastor preaching on the parable of the prodigal son might choose to begin the development of that narrative with the concept of God the Father's unconditional love as the scriptural topic, then go on to develop the subtopics with the rich and interesting materials the parable offers. There is no right or wrong organizing principle for this or any other parable. It could just as well be developed with a chronological approach, or even a spacial approach moving from the father's home, to the far country, to parts of the far country, to the trip back home, and back to the father's home. In arrangement, as in other matters, there is a broad range of rhetorical choice and great allowance for the creativity of the speaker. For example, thinking creatively about the son's journey home could be fertile soil for a lesson on sin, repentance, and grace. Indeed, the parables and most other biblical narratives offer extraordinarily rich materials that invite creative patterns of organization which may suggest creative development.

While a logical pattern of arrangement may follow either a deductive or inductive pattern, the deductive has the obvious advantage of letting the listeners know in advance just what it is that the speaker is doing. The method provides clarity and direction as the supporting materials relate naturally to the general idea from which they follow.

Inductive development proceeds from the specific to the general. Particular elements of a speech are developed before the general outline is allowed to emerge. In a sermon, for example, the pastor might heighten interest by dealing with several intriguing aspects of a text before the actual focus for the text is revealed. As you read the model sermons you will see that both Rabbi Wise and

Pastor Schofield are examples of sermons which begin with specific instances which are used to lead the listener to the scriptural topic of God's love and our reflection of that love.

The value of the inductive method stems from its rationality. The listener may be led to the acceptance of a proposition that would have raised emotional barriers if introduced without the specific instances, illustrations, and examples employed in the inductive process. The method, moreover, progresses according to a natural pattern of thought, so is easily delivered by the speaker and easily followed by the listener. See Pastor Rollefson's sermon in the appendix for an excellent example of inductive development.

The foregoing patterns are common methods of logical organization. Other useful methods which follow a logical pattern are the cause-to-effect and the extended analogy. Each is a logical pattern for which the names ascribed indicate both their form and function.

2. The Chronological Pattern: The principle of time applies to this arrangement. Narrative materials as well as discussions of a process are often best communicated when the actual sequence of events or the steps in a process are allowed to determine the order of presentation.

The chronological pattern is a simple method for arrangement and is easily followed if the speaker has organized the material into a reasonable number of time divisions. A sermon on Acts 9, Saul's journey on the Damascus road, for example, could be organized chronologically from his departure from Jerusalem to his time in Damascus. As an example of how the form suggests the substance, one can hardly reflect on the chronology without identifying who Saul was when he left Jerusalem and who he became in Damascus.

3. The Space Pattern: The principle of spacial relations may be applied as a basis for organization. Geographical subjects naturally lend themselves to such a pattern. Most speeches employing extensive description of places or objects can effectively use the space pattern. A sermon that moves from place to place might naturally use the space pattern to lend

clarity to what might be a complex relationship of places. The space pattern, moreover, often has a special appeal to the visual sense of the listener. Both the mystery and the romance of the Middle Eastern Holy Lands dotted with biblical towns and places we do not know may provide incentive for the pastor to ponder the creative use of this form of organization. Names such as the Uvda Valley, the Negev Desert, the Gush Etzion, and the Gush Dan are strange names to most, but names that will capture attention.

4. The Psychological Pattern: A psychological principle is employed when the speaker consciously orders his materials to satisfy the emotional and rational needs which arise out of a subject. In short, it is a logical approach to the psychological phenomenon of audience response. Alan Monroe used the perceived needs of the listener as key to planning the functional parts to a speech and called the system "the motivated sequence."[1] The sequence, to be adapted to the speaker's purpose, may or may not employ all five of the following steps:

1. Attention Step—to focus attention on the subject.

2. Need step—to make the audience aware of their need for information . . . or for a solution to a problem.

3. Satisfaction Step—to satisfy the need the speaker has developed.

4. The visualization step—to project into the future by visualizing the benefits of knowing, or the result of applying a solution.

5. The action step—makes a direct appeal for specific action.

The motivated sequence can easily be applied to the sermon. The first step, focusing attention on the subject (the Word for the day) is common to all patterns of organization. The second step, the need step, is particularly applicable when the scripture presents special problems, either problems in comprehending the text

1. Monroe, *Principles and Types of Speech*, 3.

or problems in the application of the text. The need step explicates those problems and the satisfaction step provides the explanation and the solutions that may be appropriate. The satisfaction step applies the scriptures to the life of the listeners. For example, the pastor might visualize for our time and place what it might mean if we invited the poor and the hungry to our banquet. The action step is appropriate when the pastor wishes to suggest specific acts for his listeners to do, or consider doing.

Patterns of organization can in themselves be helpful, both in suggesting content and in arranging the content to be most effective. The purpose for any pattern of arrangement is to give *coherence, unity, and direction* to the sermon. Those three are key words. There is nothing useful to be said about arrangement except in relation to the purpose of giving cohesiveness, unity and direction to the discourse.

The concept of giving direction to the sermon cannot be overemphasized. Whether a news report, a novel, a TV drama, a concerto, or a sermon, the reader or listener needs to sense that what is being read or heard is going somewhere. Coherence and unity are the means to the end of giving direction, and the pastor whose sermons achieve this end provides his flock a sense of participation, satisfaction, and completion.

Outlining

The easiest way to assure coherence, unity, and direction to oral discourse is by outlining. The preparation process for the Sunday sermon sketched in the introduction suggests that after you have chosen the text, settled on the purpose, and gathered supporting materials, then involve yourself in the process of outlining.

The speaker employs an outline just as an architect uses a scale drawing. While emphasis here is on the outline as an efficient tool for putting the content of a speech in order, little experience is needed to become aware that the act of creating an outline deals with the whole rhetorical process. In handling the materials of the speech through outlining the speaker not only encounters problems and makes choices about arrangement, but also about invention, style, and delivery. A consideration of two kinds of outlines suggests how the steps in speech preparation run together as one plans, through outlining, the form the speech will take.

The Working Outline: The working outline results from the speaker's first attempt to give order to the materials. The speaker now simply places all the materials under the general headings appropriate to the principle of division.

The rough outline which emerges brings together all of the potential materials of the speech and thus provides a tool with which the speaker may think through the speech/sermon.

The working outline will serve to identify faults in the speech. Organizing the materials on paper may, for example, indicate that the speaker has included more illustrative materials than are needed to develop a relatively minor aspect, or that there is too little supporting material to develop a major point. Or, the outline may call the speaker's attention to a lack of variety in the materials. The working outline may even suggest that a different principle of division should be used. In short, the working outline is as much a check on the inventive process as it is an early step in the process of arrangement.

Worth repeating is the observation that it is the working outline which serves as a tool for the speaker to work through and think through the subject. At this juncture on the way to an excellent sermon, the working outline is your best friend.

The Preparation Outline: As the working outline is revised, it develops into the preparation outline. The fully developed preparation outline is the complete plan of the speech. It differs from a manuscript in just two ways: First, the materials are in outline form to clearly indicate the relationship of the parts, the coordination and subordination of the various elements. Second, the materials may be somewhat abbreviated. For example, in Paul's speech on Mars Hill his argument for recognizing the true God might be outlined: A. What you worship as unknown I proclaim to you:

1. God/creator not live in shrine.

2. God not served by human hands, is giver of life and all things.

3. We are God's offspring not search for God in gold images.

The best method for outlining is the method that works best for you, but whether it is a bare bones outline or one quite detailed, it needs to communicate to the speaker what the main headings are, what is coordinate, and what is subordinate. It is clarity in these matters that gives the essential items of coherence, unity, and direction to your sermon.

It is useful to employ a consistent set of symbols in the outline to indicate the relationship of the parts of your sermon. Using the symbols I, A, 1, a, (1), (a), for example, the hierarchy of the symbols can be used to indicate the coordination or subordination of the content. The Roman numerals should be used to indicate the main divisions of your speech. In the simplest form that would be: I. Introduction, II. Body, and III. Conclusion. In your actual outline, the main heads should be written out to express a single idea.

The Speaker's Outline: The final preparation outline or an abbreviation of that outline can serve as the outline used when delivering the sermon, but whether the speaker prefers to speak from an outline, a manuscript, or brief notes is a very personal choice that will be discussed in the forthcoming chapter on delivery.

Transitional Elements

The completed preparation outline should insure the unity and coherence reflected by a sermon where the parts go together and one part follows smoothly from another. But the flow of the speech, the giving of direction so the listener has a sense of moving from a clear beginning to a completion, requires the employment of transitional elements which allow the speaker to move with ease from one part of the speech to another.

Transitions function as guideposts. Major transitions, those between the main parts of a speech, often review the ground the speaker has covered and indicate where the speaker is going. Minor transitional elements give unity to the development of a main part. For example, in a sermon Pastor Schofield gave on Transfiguration Sunday, direction is first given through the unity of a narrative, then the listener's attention is directed to a new approach: i.e., "I want to argue that . . ."; "Allow me to reword that." Those kinds of transitional remarks function as signposts for the listener. The speaker should not be shy about using direct, attention drawing statements, such as: "I want you to listen carefully" or "This verse has a special meaning that is often missed." For a clear example of no shyness in directing attention, nay, *commanding* attention, look to Isaiah where in each chapter the prophet prefaces important admonishments with the words *"Now hear this"* or its equivalent attention getter. You will hear the same words on any US Navy ship at sea when the quartermaster broadcasts an announcement directed to all hands: *"Now hear this."*

Transitional elements can provide an indication of concluding a part and pointing forward to where the speaker is going, i.e., "So, we have seen how David acted; now let us consider how that might apply to us."

The most effective transitions are "natural" transitions, those, like the David transition above, naturally arise from the substance of the speech rather than imposing the artificial "in the first place," "second," etc.

The Introduction

The final step in preparing the content of your sermon is the composing of the introduction and conclusion. It is worth repeating that the preparation of the introduction is the *final step*. Many speakers waste a great deal of time in the beginning mulling over how to start the speech. Introductions are to be made when one knows what is being introduced.

The primary function of the introduction is not to "get attention." As the only person standing, the pastor has a full measure of attention. Rather, the introduction functions to divert the attention naturally arising from the situation away from the speaker as a person giving a speech, and focus that attention on the subject of the speech. In short, the introduction should prepare the listener's for the substance of the speech.

A second function of the introduction is to prepare the speaker for the audience. Both experienced and inexperienced speakers find it useful to build into their introduction material which is easily delivered, so before embarking on the main body of development they may become comfortable in the speaking situation while also establishing good, direct contact with the listeners. For either purpose, the content of the introduction must be taken from materials directly relevant to the speech.

For the worship service, I call the transition from the pastor's reading of the gospel to the beginning of the sermon a *holy moment*. With the full attention of the congregation, with the gospel message clearly in mind, the pastor seizes that moment to *build a bridge from the gospel to the sermon*. In that moment, the Word is given life by the pastor.

While it is generally true that the preacher builds that bridge with an immediate reference to the Word, the text on which the sermon is based, there are two exceptions which modify the normal order. The first is the case of an extra-ordinary event such as the Boston Marathon bombing, the earthquake in Nepal, or the Charleston church tragedy. These are events that command the attention of the Christian church and demand attention from the pulpit. The second exception arises from the occasion. Bishop Boerger's sermon, for example, was given at a special service on the occasion of a seminary president's retirement, and so began with an appropriate acknowledgement.

As indicated earlier in this text, the introduction, while occupying perhaps only thirty seconds is an enormously important part of the sermon because it has the potential to completely distract the listener from the Word, rather than to focus attention on the text and give direction to its explication.

The Conclusion

Perhaps the best way to approach the subject of conclusions is to state what a conclusion is not. The conclusion is not an appendage—not a summary, recapitulation, or restatement tacked on to the end of a speech. A formal conclusion may not be required. The pastor's application of the word to the life of the listener may well serve as an effective conclusion.

While it is indeed a truism, the most fundamental observation about the content of the conclusion is that the content should function to conclude. That is, the content should provide a smooth, appropriate ending, avoiding either a sudden stop or a fumbling, dragged-out finish. Either will detract from the sermon as a whole. To avoid both, prepare the conclusion with care.

Summary

Attention to how the substance should be organized is the important second step in the preparation of a speech. Clarity and unity achieved through an appropriate pattern of organization, along with clear transitional elements, will give the speech direction and the overall orderliness will be as useful to the speaker as it is helpful to the listener.

The practice of outlining can be as useful to the speaker as the drawing of a plan is to the architect. The outline is the easiest, most effective way for the speaker to see the relationship of the parts—the coordination and subordination—as well as to see the speech as a whole. Those two abilities, to see the relationships and to see the speech as a whole, are the very best aids to effective delivery, but that is the subject of another chapter. Do remember: In speech preparation, the outline is your best friend.

The import of the introduction is enormous. A beginning that is apparently irrelevant to the Word, or faulty and distracting in other ways is probably the most common cause of failure for the sermon as a whole. The other side of the coin is that if the *holy moment* is made effective, has truly served as a bridge from *the*

Word to the substance of the sermon, then the introduction can be a highlighting preface to all that follows.

With the rhetorical choices made concerning the content of the sermon and the arrangement of that content, the speaker is ready to move on to give attention to the language of the sermon, the subject of the following chapter.

CHAPTER 3

Style

Effective Language Usage

Exegesis and theology exist because each word God speaks is at once mysterious and open ended, never completely understood.

—W. J. Burghardt, *Preaching: The Art and the Craft*

God Talk

MUCH HAS BEEN WRITTEN about "God talk." What words, what language can the mortal use to speak of the eternal? Perhaps the best we mortals can do is to learn as much about language as we can and give well informed thought to the language we use.

From ancient times writers and speakers have been concerned with style, the use of words and groups of words to add to the effectiveness of discourse. Two theories of style have always been with us; one is rhetorical, the other is not. The non-rhetorical view, called the *organic theory of composition*, has been propounded by some philosophers and literary critics since Horace argued that if the facts were in clear perspective, the words would follow naturally. The modern critic Arnold Bennett says the same when he argues that style cannot be separated from content, because an idea is conceived in the form of words.

The rhetorical view, on the other hand, argues that after the ideas are conceived, conscious attention to language will add clarity and effectiveness to the ideas expressed. Moreover, the rhetorical view goes quite beyond clarity to argue that the form itself may add effectiveness to the discourse. Kenneth Burke, in his classic *Counter-Statement* (1968), illuminates the nature of form in a manner which applies equally to written or oral discourse, to the reader or to the listener: "Form in literature is an arousing and fulfillment of desires. A work has form insofar as one part of it leads the reader to anticipate another part, to be gratified by the sequence."[1] As insightful as Burke's observation is, it deals with only a limited aspect of the appeal of form. As we have seen broader application in the previous discussions of arrangement, where the form serves to provide clarity and unity as well as providing the more psychological sequential gratification so brilliantly noted by Burke.

The rhetorical view not only argues that the *form* of expression may add or detract from the substance of the discourse, but also that principles of effective style can be formalized and learned. In the rhetorical view of style, therefore, one confronts the nature of rhetoric. Indeed, Aristotle's *Rhetoric* is based on the idea that from the observation of speechmaking principles of effectiveness can be formalized.

What then is the meaning of the rhetorical word *style*? The first step toward understanding the meaning of the term is to clarify possible ambiguities. *Elocutio*, or style, has not only been given a bad name by the philosophers but has been badly named by the rhetoricians. While the other four parts of the rhetorical canon clearly refer to processes, the term style seems to refer to a characteristic of discourse. The ambiguity has led both ancient and modern rhetoricians and critics to deal with style merely as a characteristic of discourse. In so doing, criticism becomes largely descriptive and the more difficult matter of dealing with style as a process is, for the most part, avoided.

Nevertheless, the rhetorician is concerned with style both as a characteristic and as a process in the development of discourse. A glance at early rhetorical treatises indicates the extraordinary amount of attention given to the subject of style. A consideration

---

1. Burke, *Counter-Statement*, 124.

of the substance of the teaching clarifies the nature of style and leads into the purpose for the study.

The Analysis of Style

In general, style was analyzed according to three different principles. First, style dealt with two aspects of language, words and combinations of words. Almost exclusive attention was given to groups of words called "figures of speech." A second principle of analysis centered on the virtues of the good style: clarity, appropriateness, correctness, and distinctiveness. Further analysis concerned the types of style, with distinctions made between the "plain," "middle," and "grand."

Style as a process has four functions. First, style aims to fit words and groups of words *appropriately* to the speaker, to the audience, and to the subject and circumstances of the speech. A second function is the selection of words to communicate thought *clearly*. A third function is to use language *correctly*. This third point might seem too obvious to mention except that in today's public discourse, both in public speeches and in the media, errors are frequently made, even by well educated people. Two of the most frequent errors concern pronouns. One often hears the use of *me* erroneously, as in, "He is older than me." The use of *myself* is so frequently and blatantly misused that I have advised students to simply avoid it. To say, "Give it to one of the ushers or myself," rings bells in the ears of some listeners. Another all-too-common error is the use of *and* as a verb, as in "I will try and fix it." Additionally, careful writers and speakers make proper distinctions between each and both, who and that.

Finally, but of great importance, style functions to give *distinctiveness* to the discourse. The assumption underlying the concept of distinctiveness is that *there may be a power or pleasantness in the form of expression that is distinct from the power or pleasantness of the thought expressed.* For distinctive language and expression, look no further than the psalmists, the liturgists, and the hymn writers, each of whom uses language in a manner which adds power and pleasantness to the thought expressed. For vivid images, balanced sentences, and boldness of statement, there may be no better example than Isaiah. Consider the vividness, the boldness, the form of these phrases from Isaiah which bring to life the image of peace:

> 2:4 They shall beat their swords into plowshares,
>   and their spears into pruning hooks; nation shall
>   not lift up sword against nation, neither shall they
>   learn war anymore.
> 11.6 The wolf shall live with the lamb, the leopard shall
>   lie down with the kid, the calf and the lion and the
>   fatling together, and a little child shall lead them.
> 32:2 . . . like streams of water in a dry place, like the shade
>   of a great rock in a weary land.
> 52:7 How beautiful upon the mountains are the feet of
>   the messenger who announces peace, who brings
>   good news, who announces salvation.

The whole Bible is replete with powerful language and vivid images, and so too are the hymns of the church. One of the church's newer hymns which simply explodes with strength and commitment is John Arthur's Pentecost hymn which is cited at the close of this chapter, but for now let it simply be observed that while the power of the hymn comes from the truth of its message, it is language such as *unleashed, tongues of fire, waters deep, smoldering lives,* that effectively convey that message.

Consider also the visual images in Van Dyke's classic phrases in "Joyful, Joyful, We Adore Thee": *hearts unfold like flowers before thee; melt the clouds of sin and sadness; flowering meadow-flashing sea.* The same beauty and power is in the ever-popular lines of "Amazing Grace," as the writer exhibits both boldness and simplicity in such phrases as *a wretch like me,* or simply, *the Lord has promised good to me.* For boldness of language you, like I, might quickly think of the "Lord of the Dance" with such phrases as: *I danced in the moon and the stars and the sun; they whipped and stripped and hung me high; it's hard to dance with the devil on your back.*

The liturgy is another aspect of the worship service which communicates its message in a clear, direct manner, but where we find both simple phrasing and distinctive language. The liturgy, the words of the people to their Lord, has since ancient times included the same elements of confession, prayer, praise, and thanksgiving.

Whether in the Roman Catholic Church, the Eastern Orthodox, or the Protestant denominations, the words of the liturgy clearly are the words of the people addressing their Lord. A Roman Catholic mass begins with the people's confession made to God *and* to their brothers and sisters. The gloria which follows is the people's hymn of praise: "*we* worship you, *we* give you thanks, *we* praise you." In the Great Litany of the Greek Orthodox Church the voice of the people is expressed as *us*: "In peace let *us* pray to the Lord." In the Litany of Supplication, the priest says, "Let *us* say with all our soul and all our mind, let *us* say . . ."

The voice of the people is heard in much the same way in the Protestant denominations where the worship includes the people's confession, prayers, praise, and thanksgiving, with the language of the liturgies reflecting their ancient roots. In many of those churches, new liturgies have been written, often employing plain language such as we find in the confessional portion of Marty Haugen's *Service of Light*: "We confess that we are trapped by our sin. We continue to be centered in ourselves rather than in others, and we so often fail to live up to even our own expectations of a spiritual life."[2] But all is not plain language in these new liturgies. There is distinctiveness, vividness, and power in such expressions as these: "Let my prayer rise up like incense before you"; "God of daybreak, God of shadows, come and light our hearts anew"; "Joyous light of heavenly glory, loving glow of God's own face."[3]

An observation easily drawn from this accumulation of illustrations is that a worship service built on the Word in scripture, the Word in the hymns, and the Word in liturgy is, by its nature, on an elevated level which is quite apart from the language parishioner's use and hear on an everyday basis. The sermon can draw from

2. Haugen, *Service of Light*, 1.

3. Ibid.

those materials to both enrich the sermon and bring coherence and unity to the worship experience.

Drawing appropriate sermon materials from the hymns and from the liturgy should never be simply for embellishment, but to contribute to the substance and to build unity in the overall worship service. Indeed, even though contemporary speeches and sermons are likely to employ much less embellishment than those of an earlier time, it is no less important to give thoughtful attention to one's language usage. The preacher needs to be concerned with the basic virtues of style: clarity, appropriateness, correctness, and distinctiveness. While the qualities of style remain the same whether the discourse is written or oral, it should not be concluded that the means of achieving effectiveness are the same. Speeches/sermons are intended to be heard. They must "speak well." An involved structure which is acceptable in written composition may verge on the unintelligible if used in oral discourse.

Transitional Language

To achieve clarity in oral discourse, language must function to provide verbal signposts which indicate the relationship of the parts. Think about this: To convey meaning the written word has, for example, paragraph indentations, bold headings, italics, and size of type to indicate the subordination or coordination of ideas. Even then, the writer also makes use of transitional language to enhance the clarity of the discourse.

In oral discourse the speaker must depend to a much greater extent on the effective use of transitional language to clarify the relationship of ideas. Any grammar text can supply a quantity of transitional words or phrases, and the speaker may profitably study the grammatical distinctions between the various types of connectives. The most common forms used by the speaker are these:

Transitions to Introduce an Idea:

This leads us to another . . . a further . . . a second;

Furthermore, what does this imply?

Transitions to summarize or conclude:

Those, then, are the reasons . . .

In brief, we have seen . . .

Finally; In summary; In conclusion

Before going on to . . . we may observe . . .

Transitions of logical inference:

From this, we may conclude . . .

These observations naturally lead to the conclusion . . .

Therefore, consequently

The reasonable conclusion from . . . is

In short, oral discourse presents special problems of which the speaker must be aware. The materials of the speech or sermon are often complex, yet the listener must take in the multiplicity of images and ideas *one word at a time*. It is essential, therefore, that the speaker include among those words elements which clarify relationships and give clear direction.

The Meaning of Words

In relating style to memory and delivery, oral discourse requires words whose meaning the listener can grasp immediately. The listener's problem can be compared to the hunter who shoots birds on the fly . . . they are there for a few seconds, then gone. If missed, they are not likely to return.

The speaker who recognizes the special problems inherent in oral discourse solves them, in part, by avoiding complex sentence structure and using words that are not only clear, but those which are personal, direct, forceful, and vivid. Effective speakers clear their language of trite or overly specialized language. Short clauses, blunt expressions, balanced structure, and repetition may all be used effectively. The preacher must give a special kind of attention to the matter of clarity in order to avoid the habitual use of religious terms that may be baffling to many of the listeners, terms that to the newcomer may be taken for jargon. The pastor cannot afford to assume that words such as *grace, sanctified, holy, redemption,* and a host of others will have clear meaning to the person in the pew.

The word *Trinity* is among that host of others that is so easily spoken, yet is so difficult to define, to provide clear meaning. In his homily "The Mystery of the Trinity," Fr. David Endres calls attention to the limitations of language as he tells his congregation, "We are forced to use the constructs of language to try to make sense of the complexities of God."[4]

Dana Martin's sermon on the trinity, "God In Three Persons," provides an example both poignant and humorous as he relates a childhood memory of the Oxford theologian Alister McGrath. As the congregation recited the Athanasian Creed, intoning the words "the Father incomprehensible . . . the Son incomprehensible . . . the Holy Spirit incomprehensible . . . ," a man in the congregation muttered loudly enough for all to hear, "The whole damn thing is incomprehensible."[5]

So, let that wee departure from the essentials of the matter serve as a reminder that the Word needs to be comprehended, that it is the person in the pew to whom we speak, with whom we connect if we are to communicate the meaning of the Word.

Because style serves as a means to an end, the language used must, above all, serve the ideas and purpose of the speech. Of course, the language must be appropriate to the speaker, the listeners, and the occasion, but the relationship of the words to the speaker's purpose is even more important. The critic Maria Nichols describes so clearly how language functions as the speaker employs words as "a system of symbols designed to evoke certain images favorable to the accomplishment of his purpose and to prevent certain other images from arising." Simply put, she asks: What are the words doing?[6] Or, paraphrasing the words of Kenneth Burke, how is *language acting to obtain its ends?*

4. Endres, "Mystery of the Trinity."

5 Cox, *Best Sermons,* 112.

6. Nichols, *Rhetoric and Criticism,* 91.

The Meaning of Meaning

Words function to communicate meaning . . . and that seems simple enough until one confronts the question of the meaning of meaning. Nothing is more personal than meaning. The meaning of words is in people. To illustrate, let us consider the meaning of the simple four-letter word *base*: The chemist, the politician, the choir director, the baseball player, and the Army private will each give you a different meaning, in accordance with *who they are and what they do*. Accordingly, the speaker, and most especially the preacher, must give clear thought to what the words of the sermon might be doing, well beyond simply avoiding vagueness and ambiguity.

The Distinctive Style

The speaker's style is also a very personal matter. There is some truth in the old saying: "Style is the man." But it is not the essential qualities of clarity, correctness, and appropriateness that individualize a speaker's style. Those are qualities that should be exhibited by all speakers. It is the *distinctiveness* of the style that sets a speaker apart.

The whole matter of distinctiveness as a quality of one's language usage, or one's style, is far less obvious and far more tenuous to grasp than such qualities as clarity or appropriateness. Distinctiveness is far easier to detect than to describe or define.

And, because we are talking about a quality, there is a subjective nature to whatever we might say about distinctiveness. Indeed, in their landmark book on written style, the authors Strunk and White began their discussion of distinctive style with the observation, "Here we leave solid ground. Who can confidentially say what ignites a certain combination of words, causing them to explode in the mind?"[7]

Nevertheless, we do recognize distinguished style when we hear it. Who can forget Bonhoeffer's provocative observation that

7. Strunk and White, *Elements of Style*, 66.

"we build him a temple, but we live in our own houses"?[8] Stanford University's campus pastor, Richard Foster, illuminated his thoughts on the poetry of the spirit with the distinctive words of a Chinese proverb: "A bird doesn't sing because it has an answer; it sings because it has a song." Consider both the thought and the balanced structure of Thomas Aquinas: "To one who has faith, no explanation is necessary. To one without faith, no explanation is possible." A gay seminarian, contemplating the progression of the church, states his view in clear and vivid language: "God's power to breathe life is always more powerful than our human capacity to suffocate ourselves." Finally, consider the profundity in Mahatma Gandhi's simple expression: "The law of love could be best understood and learned through little children."

There is little commonality in either form or substance in those five examples, but one thing they exhibit in common is distinguished thought.

There is a relationship. The idea that a distinguished speaking style begins with distinguished thought brings us back to the non-rhetorical view that "style is the man." There is some truth to that view. The person with a liberal education . . . the person who knows something of history, art, psychology, literature, music, philosophy, physics, and politics, along with current affairs and various cultures, has a foundation for both distinguished thought and distinguished speech. Nevertheless, we all know bright, superbly educated people who are, in effect, disabled, unable to make their potentially valuable contribution to the civil discourse. A former Stanford student, Robert Sayler, suggests the scope of that problem in his recent book titled *Tongue-Tied America*.[9]

How then is an effective, perhaps distinctive style achieved? There is no clear and easy path, no North Star to the attainment of excellence in language usage. But many speakers have learned to use language to achieve a style which is at once appropriate and clear, pleasing and persuasive. Mind you, we are not talking about

8. Bonhoeffer, "Jesus Christ and the Essence of Christianity," lecture, December 11, 1928, Barcelona.

9. Sayler and Shadel, *Tongue-Tied America*.

Lincoln, Churchill, or John F. Kennedy, but speakers like you. It should be noted, however, that one's own language usage is naturally enriched by observing distinctive language usage such as one finds in Lincoln's Second Inaugural Address, Churchill's WWII speeches, Kennedy's Inaugural Address, or in the powerful and beautiful phrases of the Reverend Martin Luther King.

In response to the question of how speakers achieve effectiveness in style, writers have traditionally recognized three sources: natural endowment, experience, and training. Even Horace and Plato, after venturing organic theories of composition, recognized the necessity of both natural gifts and training: "If you fall short in either of these you will to that extent be defective."[10]

As noted, there are no easy steps to achieve a distinctive style in oral discourse. Indeed, the process never ends as long as one has the ability to learn. There are however, some practical steps in the learning process.

First, a speaker should analyze one's own language habits. Give conscious attention to oral expression: weed out clichés, trite expressions, and incorrect usage. Second, cultivate an even better vocabulary. And third, the preacher should cultivate the habit of reviewing and perhaps revising the language of the sermon. Whether one has a manuscript or a preparation outline, the speaker should constantly seek the word that *best evokes the response intended*.

There are two ideas which are basic to achieving an effective, distinctive speaking style. First, the achievement of excellence in language usage must be based on a mastery of the other parts of rhetoric. Only the speaker who has solved the problems of invention, arrangement, and delivery will be free to devote attention to style. It is then that style may become an important *means* to the end of giving effectiveness to the speaker's ideas. The sophist is the speaker for whom style is an end in itself. Removed from the urgency of subject matter, style tends toward decoration and virtuosity. The study of rhetoric, except as a means to an end, tends to become a study of style. Style as a means is a central idea in

10. Plato, *Phaedrus*.

rhetorical studies. In sum, *let natural growth, even if slow, have its way. Do not attempt to affect a distinctive style.*

Underlying all studies of style is the idea that the speaker must know how language functions. The speaker, perhaps even more the pastor, must learn to treat words as *symbols*. See, for example, the introduction to I. A. Richards's *Philosophy of Rhetoric* for an excellent primer on the symbolic nature of language. To appreciate the symbolic nature of speech, one must first abandon the idea that *a word* has *a meaning*. Reference has been made, for example, to the wide differences in meaning of the simple word *base, with the meaning dependent on the person using the word.* It is even more perplexing to state the meaning of more evocative words such as liberal, extremist, activist, sanctified, religious, glorified, and blessed.

While the disciplined study of meaning has largely been a contemporary phenomenon, the study of word meaning is far from new. William Hazlitt, the eighteenth-century English critic and writer, observed that language is the common denominator of thought; it holds and expresses only that pool of ideas which we possess in common. The modern critic Kenneth Burke put it another way as he too observes that the meaning of words lies in people. Meaning is static insofar as people are the same; meaning is dynamic because of our differences.

In sum, modern studies of language usage have focused on the functioning of words in discourse. The trend has been away from the analysis and description of stylistic forms to an approach which centers attention on functional aspects of word usage. Yet, the central question is what it always was: Are words being used effectively to achieve the speaker's purpose?

In regard to the language of the sermon, the pastor has special problems and special opportunities. With regard to problems, it should be recognized that the pastor cannot avoid the use of many highly evocative words, words that can evoke vivid images in the minds of the listeners. God talk includes words like *salvation, holy, heaven, the spirit, forgiveness, the community of saints, faith, grace, love, judgment, life everlasting.* The pastor who knows the congregation and understands the symbolic nature of language will likely turn the problem of evocative words into an asset.

A special opportunity for the sermon builder who wishes to achieve distinctiveness in language usage is that much of the material that might well be employed in the sermon is already on the highest level of distinctiveness. There is a readily available treasure trove of precious items on which any pastor may draw. For example, with reference to the care of God's creation, Joseph Sittler turns to the beautiful and powerful hymn "This Is My Father's World," as he observes, "This is, indeed, my Father's world. We sing the hymn, but we do not preach the substance."[11] A perusal of John Arthur's powerful hymn for Pentecost might well inspire several sermons.

Consider the thought and the language:

> Spirit of God, unleashed on earth, with rush of wind and
> roar of flame; With tongues of fire men spread good
> news;
> Earth, kindling blazed its loud acclaim.
> You came in pow'r, your Church was born; O Holy Spirit,
> come again! Raise up new saints from waters deep;
> Let new tongues hail the risen Lord.
>
> Let new lips, tasting victory won, inspire our hearts
> grown
> cold with fear; Revive in us baptismal grace,
> And fan our smoldering lives to flame.[12]

So, know the liturgies, old and new. Read the liturgies and the hymns with the kind of attention you give your Bible. Reading and pondering on the substance of the liturgy and the words of the hymns will empower you, and thus empower your sermons, and thus empower your listeners. And the empowerment of the listener, as the teenagers say, "Is what it's all about." Indeed, the end, the purpose of every sermon, is to empower the listener.

11. Sittler, *Gravity and Grace*, 12.

12. Arthur, "Spirit of God Unleashed on Earth," in the *Lutheran Book of Worship*, 387.

The suggestion here is that when one considers the quality, profundity, and beauty of the scriptures, the liturgies, and the hymns . . . and the pastor's opportunity to draw on all such wisdom and beauty of the ages, it may be difficult after all to avoid excellence and distinctiveness as one builds a sermon in one's own style, but from the richness of those holy materials.

Summary

Style concerns the use of language in discourse. The rhetorical approach to style argues that, beyond the words themselves, the *form* of expression can add to the effectiveness, principles of effective style can be formalized and learned, and beyond treating style simply as a characteristic of discourse there is much to be learned from treating style as a *process* which has four functions: to provide to the discourse correctness, clarity, appropriateness, and distinctiveness.

Problems inherent in *oral discourse* create a need for attention to special "road signs" and transitional elements to direct the listener. Problems inherent in the nature of language require attention to both the *symbolic* nature of language and to the question of word *meaning*. In the entire chapter's discussion of style, the pastor may note that for the builder of sermons there are special problems and special opportunities. My belief is that the quantity and quality of distinctive materials available to the preacher weigh the scales in the direction of special opportunities.

Now, after many hours of preparation to find, select, and absorb the content, to organize it most effectively, and to make language choices to achieve clarity and distinctiveness, and many more hours allowing all of that to soak in subconsciously, you are ready to spend a relatively few minutes in the pulpit or near it to present yourself and your sermon to your congregation. You need to be able to deliver the fruits of your labor. The next chapter aims to help you do that.

CHAPTER 4

Delivery and Memory

Knowing the word is not enough . . . the preacher
must be able to communicate it.

—George Campbell, *Pulpit Eloquence*

Importance of Delivery

THE FIRST THING ONE needs to know about delivery, the fourth part of rhetoric, is how important it is. Up until now you have been working alone to develop your sermon for your congregation. Now the music, the liturgy, the reading of the Word culminates in "The Holy Moment" when the preacher shares the sermon with the congregation. After all the effort that has gone before, the congregation shares only in what is to come, the sermon as it is delivered that Sabbath day. A sermon delivered well will enhance the content, but even the best prepared sermon with the finest content may not reach the listener if the delivery is ineffective.

There are two ingredients to effective delivery and the pastor must bring both to the pulpit. The first is a right attitude; the second is right preparation. Wrong attitudes include being self-conscious or material conscious rather than *idea conscious* and *audience conscious*. A right attitude is a natural result of your having a clear purpose, confidence in your materials, and a genuine desire to *connect* with your congregation to communicate your message. While it should go without saying, *your message* is italicized only to emphasize the difficulties in presenting someone else's ideas, or even your own ideas from a previous time. The *process of preparation* is an essential part of bringing vitality to the sermon. There is an intimate relationship between thought and speech. Fluent thought, clear thought, *your* thoughts lead to fluent, clear extempore speech.

Those elements of right attitude and clear purpose, especially your burning desire to connect with your people, your flock, lead to the right spirit within you which can empower you and which can and should be absorbed by those to whom you speak. And, in this act of delivering the Word to your people, the preacher reveals himself or herself, a clear and immediate revelation of the *ethos* of the speaker. In the contemporary language of the teenager, the message is to *be real*, the same advice given centuries ago by Quintilian in his *Institutes of Oratory* as he insisted that effective delivery, true delivery, must reveal the true person. So, be real. Be yourself.

The second ingredient, preparation, is basic to a right attitude and is what provides clarity of purpose and confidence in your materials. With those thoughts as background, let us move on to some of the nuts and bolts relevant to delivery as a means to add effectiveness to the sermon.

Types of Delivery

The terms widely used to distinguish different types of delivery generally include the impromptu speech, the off-the-cuff remarks given with no preparation. While the impromptu mode is never relevant to the sermon, a few thoughts might be offered on the subject because pastors are public figures who are frequently called upon, whether at a PTA meeting or a Women's Guild, to "*say a few words.*" The cardinal rule for impromptu speaking is: Never give a truly impromptu speech. That is, anticipate those occasions when you might be called upon. A few moments thinking of some appropriate remarks ahead of the occasion may save some embarrassing moments later on.

So, putting the impromptu aside, the three types of delivery are the memorized, reading from manuscript, and extemporaneous, or extempore.

Memorized

While the memorized speech is generally viewed as a thing of the past, it should be observed that though rarely done, the speech delivered from memory can be effective if done well.

A memorized speech is often less hesitant and smoother than a speech read from manuscript, but it can be equally dismal if the speaker simply mouths what he has memorized without a lively awareness of the meaning of the words memorized, along with a lively sense of audience contact. On the other hand, many well-known speeches have been delivered from memory. It all depends on how one memorizes. If the speaker keeps an alert mind, visualizes the speech as a whole, has memorized thoroughly so the mind is not groping for half-forgotten words, then the speaker can proceed confidently while connecting with the listeners. The memorized speech may be useful as a means to improve delivery for it enables one to give a large measure of attention to articulation, use of the voice (modulation of rate, pitch, and volume), and adjustment to the speaking situation.

More relevant to contemporary public speaking is the memorization of parts of a speech. For example, instead of reading an extended quotation, a short poem, or verses from a hymn, speaking them from the head and heart may add a fresh dimension that can be highly effective.

In sum, the memorized speech is ordinarily not well suited to contemporary public speaking, and probably not at all to the sermon. So, while rare, there may be the occasional person who can deliver a memorized sermon effectively.

Manuscript

The speech read from a manuscript has its place in public address, but a limited place. Public officials sometimes read speeches because the importance of the subject demands strict accuracy and because a misstatement might have serious repercussions. In short, the occasion determines the choice of a manuscript; it is not chosen because it is the best method for communication.

Indeed, reading from a manuscript is never the best means of communication whatever the speech occasion, and certainly not for the pastor who must be fully involved in the double task of presenting solid content while engaging with the listener in a direct, sincere, personal manner. The most discouraging comment on the use of the manuscript may be the observation that there are just two reasons for a speaker to read from a manuscript: Either the speaker does not understand the subject, or the speaker does not believe in what is being spoken.

That said, some speakers find it useful to write out their speech in the process of preparation, so a completed manuscript is the result. That manuscript can be a beneficial means to visually review the speech as a whole and perhaps edit such details as word choice and transitional elements. Even when one has happily settled on a final manuscript, the speaker should not be so committed to it as to obviate the spontaneity often triggered by the energy generated by a lively speaker-audience connection, a connection difficult to achieve if attention is largely devoted to the manuscript. The communication problem with the use of a manuscript is in the *reading* of the manuscript in place of a more direct means of communication. In a rhetorical sense, reading is not speaking.

A well-developed manuscript can, however, be used effectively in the process of delivering the speech. Much like other speakers use notes, some speakers bring to the podium or pulpit a manuscript with which they are very familiar. It probably has some underlining, some red arrows, some notes in the margins. It serves as a roadmap, not as finished prose to be read. So, the last word on manuscripts is: Use them if you must, but never let the manuscript use you.

Extemporaneous

Extemporaneous delivery is the type used in almost all public speaking and in almost all of our daily conversation. A mistaken idea is that extempore speech requires less preparation than other types of delivery. Not so! The extempore speech is thoroughly prepared even though the exact language is not set. The words, most of them, are manufactured as one speaks, just as in our daily conversation. The difference between our extempore speaking in everyday conversation and the extempore speaking used in a formal speech situation is a difference in *degree*, not a difference in *kind*.

As a result of the thorough preparation and of not having to focus throughout the speech on particular phrases or words, the speaker is free to be idea conscious and audience conscious, the winning combination for the most effective communication. The real, authentic connection with the audience can only be achieved with extempore delivery, and that high level of achievement requires both practice and experience. It is a level of excellence worth aiming for, working on, and waiting for. It will come.

A few extempore speakers, pastors included, speak entirely without notes, or appear to do so. Most speakers, and certainly most pastors, do utilize notes. Perhaps the best advice to less experienced speakers regarding notes is to experiment with different forms to find what is best for you. To all speakers: Use what is most useful and comfortable.

If one is using a pulpit or podium, notes can be on a full-size 8 1/2 x 11 sheet of paper, but half that size would probably be more practical. The pastor who speaks simply from the front of the sanctuary sans podium or pulpit gains the advantages of both proximity and movement, both potentially important factors as one seeks to connect with an audience. Some of these speakers use no notes, but most have at least a few 3 x 5 or 4 x 6 cards for reference.

Whatever the form of the notes, the important thing to the speaker is that the notes are clear and can be used with ease. The important thing to the audience is *how* the notes are used. Notes should never be used self-consciously as though there was something wrong with having them. One should avoid peeking at one's notes with furtive glances. Look at your notes. Use them, even pausing to look at them.

The most common fault with the use of notes is their overuse. Time and again the audience sees the speaker, the pastor, glancing at the notes every four or five seconds, and often in places where everyone knows the notes could not possibly be needed. The fluent articulation of ideas is easily interrupted by the overuse of notes and the head bobbing that goes with it. Such overuse can be due to lack of preparation or lack of familiarity with ones notes, but it usually is not. It is more likely just a habit, a bad habit. Some attitude adjustment, plus practice with a mirror, will probably set things straight.

Overcoming the habitual looking at one's notes is of special import for the pastor because of the distinctive nature of the sermon content. Talking about the Word of God, faith, grace, and belief demands direct, sincere, uninhibited connection between speaker and listener, between pulpit and pew. Having to read or consult one's notes about what one believes is not in the nature of this speech act.

In sum, be comfortable with your notes and use them judiciously. Never allow your notes to get between you and your audience.

The Mechanics of Delivery

Our attention to delivery would be incomplete without attention to the mechanics of delivery. Indeed, the production of speech requires a cooperative effort on the part of more than half the muscles in the human body. Most of the human frame is involved in speechmaking. That is why it is tiring, and all the more so if muscular tension is involved.

Those with an academic background in speech communication sometimes approach the mechanical aspects of speechmaking with a degree of hesitancy; much like a modern pharmacist might approach the subject of the cure-all snake oil, or other such nineteenth-century remedies. There is some warrant for this apprehension, as the nineteenth-century elocutionists tended to focus on the mechanics of delivery to the extent that the speech might become a mechanical performance where a variety of gestures were learned along with other artificial manipulations of the voice and body. The elocutionary influence was strong even into the twentieth century until James Winans's classic 1928 text *Public Speaking* placed speech communication studies firmly on an academic track, a return to the classical rhetorical tradition with its emphasis on the content and purpose of the speech.[1] Nevertheless, speakers throughout the ages have had to devote conscious attention to the mechanics. Voice, diction, gesture, and movement are part of the rhetorical act and not to be ignored.

After listening to a fluent speaker one often wonders how much of that fluency is owing to native ability and how much to training and practice. There may be "born speakers," but most of us have to take a more tedious route to develop effectiveness in delivery. To achieve competence, as with the other parts of rhetoric, one needs to know what one is doing and then to work at it diligently. In his unpublished *Handbook* prepared for his Stanford students in 1927 Lee Emerson Bassett compares the task of the inexperienced speaker to that of the beginning pianist who struggles to control stiff and uncertain fingers, until eventually they become free and sure and instantly responsive. In the same way, the speaker needs to devote effort to control the instruments of expression, the voice and body, until, like the skilled pianist, thought and action becomes one and there is a wholeness and naturalness to the form of expression.

1. Winans, *Speech-Making*, 112.

Voice

Few of us make full use of our voice. Because the sounds we normally make seem loud enough we wrongly assume that the same sounds will be appropriate in public speaking. Whether or not amplification is used, one should determine how much volume is required for a certain space and should practice using the voice and projection that will be suitable. If a person can develop the appropriate volume and learn to project the voice, one will have at least one of the essentials of effective delivery. With practice and speaking experience the person gains in resonance, richness, and control of voice.

Breathing

Learning to breathe properly should go along with learning to use the voice. Through practice one can modify, if not change one's breathing habits so that deep breathing and muscular control become natural. The dropping of sentence endings is a common fault even among experienced speakers. While the fault may be habitual, it is more likely due to a loss of focus, or to fatigue. The most convenient means to learn breath control is through the reading of poetry aloud. Reading the psalms aloud will serve you well.

Articulation

Just as an actor must apply makeup in order to appear natural under stage lighting, so must a speaker enunciate vowels and consonants more vigorously when speaking to an audience. When a speaker carries halfhearted articulation before an audience, many of the words uttered will be lost. Articulating clearly requires physical effort involving the tongue, teeth, lips, and jaw. If a speaker has clearly enunciated words like compassion, stewardship, congregation, and devotion and has used the articulators and spoken slowly, one will be conscious of active exertion. The acquisition of clear enunciation first requires awareness and sensitivity, and may require disciplined practice.

Pronunciation and Usage

Pronunciation, usage, and grammar are conventions. The best rule is to let the usage of educated people be your guide. The speaker must use the living language, which is not to say that the pastor need employ the most popular language of the day.

Pauses and Rate

Pauses are to the speaker what punctuation is to the writer. Pauses indicate the divisions and units of thought. The inexperienced speaker cannot bear to pause. The silence of the room is so painful that one hurries on, running sentences and words together. The experienced speaker makes purposeful use of the pause.

Overly rapid speech is a common hindrance to communication. Normal speech is about 120 words per minute. Even an interested and sympathetic audience may be simply turned off by a speaker who significantly exceeds that norm. The rate of delivery must be such as to be comfortably assimilated by the listener. The nature of the sermon content suggests the inappropriateness of a rapid delivery. As with the purposeful use of the pause, changes in the rate of delivery can be an effective means of communication.

Eye Contact

Effective speakers quickly establish good eye contact, just as one would in normal conversation. The eye contact should take in the entire audience so that one seems to be speaking directly to each member. With a little experience, this kind of visual connection with the listeners will become habitual. Direct contact with the eyes holds attention, gives the speaker confidence, and gives both the speaker and the listener a lively sense of connection.

Gesture and Movement

The impulse to gesture is deep-seated and never ought to be rigidly checked. Gesturing is a natural part of speaking; everyone gestures whether one thinks about it or not. The best advice about gesturing is not to be concerned about it. When the speaker learns how to put the speech together and thus gains confidence, the inhibitions that get in the way of natural gestures will disappear. The speaker will find that gesturing and walking about a bit will reduce muscular tension. Most difficulties of manner and bearing derive from tension of the muscles, which in turn derives from anxiety and lack of mental control. Once again, the solution to even these kinds of physical impediments is grounded in preparation. If the speaker is sufficiently the master of the subject matter and is eager to speak, one's mental confidence will help impart the muscular control needed and will lead to natural gestures and natural movement.

Memory

Memory is a ubiquitous topic of interest and concern to everyone and is also an elusive topic. Gerhard Frost begins his wonderfully rich *Meditations on the Later Years* with words from the popular song "Try to Remember": "Deep in December it's nice to remember, without a hurt the heart is hollow." "Memory" was also one of the never-to-be-forgotten songs from Frank Lloyd Webber's *Cats*: "Midnight, not a sound from the pavement, Has the moon lost her memory?"

The concept of memory and the process of remembering is deeply embedded in our music and poetry as well as in our religion with its covenants, commandments, and sacraments.

The ancients had a more practical reason to attend to memory as a part of rhetoric. While Pericles's well-known Funeral Oration was uncharacteristically brief, many of the speeches of the best known classical orators, Greek or Roman, were extremely long, especially by modern standards. Demosthenes's speech "On the Crown," known as a masterpiece of classical oratory, has over twenty-seven thousand words, so at a normal rate of speaking it would take nearly four hours to deliver. The ancient orator's need for a method to remember the full content of the speech led to the Greek's development of a systematic way to aid recall. The Greek poet Simonides is credited with developing the first *mnemonic* system, a method of imagery using specific places or *loci* to store information which is then recalled as the speaker mentally moves from place to place. The system was later described by the Roman orator/rhetorician Cicero, and was developed into elaborate techniques in both the Middle Ages and Renaissance. Current interest in mnemonics has resulted in a considerable body of research. In 1967 Gerald Miller found that the use of a mnemonic system increased student test scores by up to 77 percent. Joshua Foer's 2011 book, *Moonwalking with Einstein*, explains that mnemonic expertise is based on the creation of vivid images in the mind. So, for the past twenty-five hundred years, from Simonides to Joshua Foer, systems for remembering are grounded in the creation of images.

While the whole subject of memory is interesting in itself, it should be obvious that it is of far less importance to the modern speaker than to his or her predecessors. For today's pastor, the sermon does not require memorization. While the pastor should be able to visualize the basic outline of the sermon, the memorization of the entire sermon should be avoided.

One aspect of memory that is particular to the clergy is their familiarity with Scripture. While one would not expect the clergy to memorize the Bible, the pastor should be so familiar with Scripture that it becomes second nature to see the text for the day in relationship to other related texts. This kind of perception of the relationship of texts can contribute much to the meaning of the text, enrich the sermon content, and enlarge the congregation's familiarity and understanding of the Bible.

The Listener's Memory

Another aspect of memory as it relates to the sermon is a consideration of the listener's memory. What makes a sermon memorable?

In this case the easy answer is the right one: The sermon people will listen to and remember is the sermon that has solid content, has something important to say, and says it in an interesting, clearly organized, and engaging way. More specifically, as an aid to the listener's memory, there will be places in the sermon that the pastor is especially passionate about or regards as especially important. These can be pointed out, verbally underlined: "I want each one of you to underline this next idea in your mind" or "I want you to remember this." In sum, the pastor should see the sermon as a whole and help the audience in every way to be able to do the same.

For the person in the pulpit there is another trinity to think about: The speaker, the speech/sermon/homily, and the listener. A Stanford University brochure for a communications workshop highlighted the statement that "in an age of automation and mass communications, *The Listener*, as an actively thinking individual, has often been forgotten." For the preacher, it is often good to think of communicating to a *listener* rather than to a congregation. This focus on the listener should begin as one prepares the sermon . . . and certainly continue as one delivers it.

While it has always been a challenge for any speaker to fully engage the mind of the listener, the 21st century person in the pew presents new problems. It is far more difficult today to present an attention getting, attention holding, and memorable sermon to a listener who is of a new generation, raised with new technology, drowning in a sea of media images, and accustomed to instant gratification via the latest version of the iphone. You can safely assume a short attention span.

The contemporary preacher is aware of those difficulties and that awareness should sharpen one's sensitivity to what it is that makes a person listen, remember, and respond. Attention determines response. Attention also determines what one remembers. The materials discussed previously under invention, arrangement, and style are all relevant. Items the psychologists relate to memory can be identified here: Frequency, vividness, and the unusual.

As for frequency, its rhetorical application is simply that repetition aids memory. Important ideas, key concepts in a sermon can be and probably should be repeated. Vividness can be achieved in concrete examples and descriptions as well as in illustrations that actually illustrate, actually paint a mental image. The unusual can be achieved either with content that is striking beyond the ordinary, or with language that exhibits the same qualities.

As mentioned earlier, the concrete descriptive content of a sermon on the Twenty-Third Psalm is clearly remembered, although heard as an undergraduate student attending a college chapel service. Another example of unusual, distinctive language which makes the idea unforgettable is the language from a Mother's Day sermon given many years ago by Bishop Fulton Sheen. Striking in form and substance, his observation was, "Every virgin longs to be a mother, and every mother longs to be a virgin."[2] That concept required some explanation, but you can be sure that it was a distinctive, attention-getting statement not to be forgotten.

And not to be forgotten are the words of the superb layman/speaker/teacher/preacher Dr. Leo Bustad as he reminded his listeners that the Lord has given us one mouth and two ears, a fact that should have clear implications for us. In his wonderfully instructive book on Christian fellowship, Dietrich Bonhoeffer tells us that "the first service one owes to others in the fellowship is to listen."[3] And so it is . . . the listener is important, the never-to-be-forgotten third part of that communication trinity of speaker, speech/sermon/homily, and listener.

Summary

No matter how excellent the content, the goods must be delivered if the sermon is to have its intended effect. The fluency of the gifted orator is not needed. The pastor who is well prepared and graces the sermon scene with a right spirit that genuinely connects with the people in the pew will have good delivery. An authentic

2. Sheen, "Virgin Who Is a Mother," 5.
3. Bonhoeffer, *Life Together*, 97.

connection on both the idea level and personal level will bring a quality of vitality to the sermon, the pastor, and the congregation.

Most pastors will speak extemporaneously with notes, but even if a manuscript is used, it will most likely be used as a guide, not a document to be read, so the delivery is most likely extempore. While the speaker needs to attend to the mechanics of delivery, including voice, articulation, gesture, and movement, each of those elements should be governed by the content. All should flow naturally from what is being said. Although memorization may play little part in contemporary speechmaking, the speaker, through memorization or otherwise, needs to see the speech as a whole and be completely familiar and comfortable with the notes or outline being used.

Most important, delivery is but a means to an end. If the aim of public speaking is communication, then the test of good delivery is the effectiveness with which it transmits the speaker's ideas to an audience. That which advances the speaker's purpose is good; that which hinders it is bad.

Rather than ending on that pragmatic note, this text ends where it began: *In the beginning was the Word, and now the articulation of the Word is in your hands.* The delivery of the Word to your people can be enhanced by your knowledge of rhetorical principles, the means to effective communication. The aim of this book has been to apply rhetorical principles ranging from Aristotle and Augustine to Kenneth Burke and I. A. Richards to the task of sermon building. May it serve as a helpful guide and companion in your journey.

APPENDIX A

Sample Sermons

THE SERMONS AND PORTIONS of sermons included here have been selected both for their quality and for the diversity they represent. The diversity reflected in these sermons should underline the fact that there is no single "right way" to form a sermon. Harking back to this text's introduction, "A sermon is, first of all, a person speaking." Your sermon is your sermon.

One important disclaimer to be noted is that because these sermons are presented in manuscript form (How else?), it does not mean that they were delivered from a manuscript. Indeed, in the case of one of the complete sermons included here, the pastor uses no notes at all in the actual delivery. (The manuscript was prepared later for another purpose.) In another of the complete sermons, notes were used, and then the manuscript prepared for inclusion here.

While there is a broad range of diversity in these models, one important characteristic in which there is uniformity is in their fidelity to the Word, and the application of the Word to the lives of the people. These models are also similar in being good examples for the rhetorical principles discussed in the text. Some of those principles will be noted, but in addition to those observations it is hoped that the reader will find profit and pleasure in doing what Aristotle did: Observe, learn from others, and formulate useful concepts for your own effectiveness.

"Finding God at the Heart of Things"

Readings: Exodus 16:2–4, 12–15; Psalm 78;
Ephesians 4:17, 20–24; John 6:24–35

Fr. Tim Valentine, SJ
Amityville, New York

THE INTRODUCTION employs a marvelously rich, descriptive illustration to lead to the Gospel text and also to the embracing of the concept of seeing God and finding God at the heart of all things. Fr. Valentine's homily not only addresses all the scriptural texts for the day but also refers back to the previous week's account of the feeding of the multitudes, relates that to the text for the day, and then provides a preview of the texts and themes for the next three weeks.

The concept of God's presence for us, and the concept of the "real presence" of Christ in the Eucharist are not easy concepts to communicate or to grasp. The clarity of thought and expression exhibited in this homily is achieved with clear language, clear transitions, clear examples, and clear explanations.

Readers of this homily might well be astonished at how much substance is given in so few words. If delivered at a normal rate the presentation would be about eight minutes. The brevity is partly due to a clear focus consistently maintained.

Finding God at the Heart of Things

What do Pope Francis and an entire generation of chefs, bakers, and "foodies" have in common? A favorite film, Gabriel Axel's *Babette's Feast* (1987), based on a novel by Isak Dinesen. Set in a 19th-century Danish fishing village, the story, filled with biblical/religious imagery, depicts the life of a small Protestant sect founded by a venerable Lutheran pastor, and cared for after his death by his pious daughters Martine (Luther?) and Phillipa (Melancthon?). Into this world of earnest, severe human beings, enter two exotic visitors from Paris. These include opera singer Achilles Papin and, years later, a chef named Babette, who comes seeking refuge from the civil unrest that claimed her family. In appreciation for their kindness to her, Babette begs her hosts for the privilege of cooking a traditional French dinner for the community. Her offer is met with the same suspicion that had previously greeted Papin's musical artistry. After all, overindulgence of the senses can lead to sin: a love song is just one step away from immorality, and sumptuous dining from gluttony and drunkenness. Almost despite themselves, the devout believers and their guests—twelve in all—relent, and find their lives transformed by the meal. The piece de resistance of the dinner is Babette's signature dish: *cailles en sarcophage* ("quail in sarcophagus"), a small partridge-like bird baked in pastry. The effect of the food and wine goes beyond their merely aesthetic properties. A sensuous experience acts as the medium through which ineffable beauty—whose source is God—draws the human heart to itself. Indeed, according to one guest (a cultivated military officer), Babette's meal brings about "a kind of love affair between heaven and earth." So, too, among the guests: frayed relationships are healed, isolation gives way to tender affection, and the love of God binds together the hearts of all. In the words of the scriptures, "Taste and see the goodness of the Lord" (Ps 34:8).

This beautiful film, much like today's scriptures, embodies what theologian David Tracy calls the "analogical imagination" underlying the Catholic sacramental system. According to this idea, the material world has the capacity to convey the grace of

God. Of course, the Bible does not argue this point by making technical, metaphysical distinctions. Instead, it uses concrete realities—people, places, and things—to show that God becomes tangibly present to believers, giving them life in this world, and in the next. With this in mind, we turn to today's scriptures.

The first reading from the book of Exodus describes the people of Israel engaging in typical human behavior. Having witnessed firsthand the power of God who freed them from soul-crushing slavery in Egypt, they fail to trust him when it comes to more mundane matters. As once they complained to God and Moses about Pharaoh's unreasonable demands during their slavery, so now they are overcome by fear of the journey in the desert and, subsequently, thirst, hunger, the quality of food. In short, the people fail to trust that God is concerned with their physical well-being, to say nothing of their loftier aspirations. St. Ambrose (*On the Mysteries*, #44–48), points out that in sending food from heaven—quail (flesh) and manna (bread)—God attends to the basic needs of his children, while at the same time foreshadowing a food that would nourish them for eternal life. Today, Christians interpret this "heavenly bread," or "food of angels," of which the psalmist sings (Ps 78:25), as the sacrament of the Eucharist.

The first reading, especially its theme of trust in divine providence, is the context for today's Gospel. Following last Sunday's account of the miraculous feeding of the crowds, the following Sundays concern its deeper meaning: this week and next, the importance of faith in Christ, and the next two, what Catholics call the "real presence" of Christ in the Eucharist.

St. Augustine comments that, just as he had satisfied them with bread, so now Jesus desires to feed the people with his word. In order for this to happen, he tries to awaken in them a genuine hunger for eternal life, not simply the prolongation of earthly existence. Yet, as is typical of the dialogues in the Fourth Gospel, Jesus and those with whom he converses are speaking on different levels. For example, the Samaritan woman earlier speaks of "water" in an earthly sense as what sustains physical life, while Jesus speaks of "living water," or faith, which is necessary for salvation. Just so, the people today are drawn to Jesus, not because the "sign" of the loaves arouses their faith in the one on whom God has set his "seal" (or what St. Hilary calls God's "perfect impression"), but by the prospect of another meal, after which they would again hunger.

Thus, Jesus directs the people to "work for . . . the food which endures for eternal life," and not settle for lesser things. Work, in this sense, is not the kind of labor associated with tilling the soil, gathering grain, or baking loaves, but of "believing in the Son of Man." Augustine observes the enormous difference between merely "believing" Jesus, that is, intellectually grasping what he says, and "believing in" him, i.e., trusting, honoring, and loving him. Surely, a devil can do the former, but only the disciple is capable of the latter. For Augustine, to be so caught up in earthly, passing things that one fails to appreciate—and respond to—the inner realities they convey, is to make a tragic blunder.

In the weeks ahead, the Church asks us to meditate on the sacramental presence of Christ in the Eucharist, which is neither a merely physical reality, nor purely a symbol. The creative tension between the interior act of "believing in" Jesus, and the concrete act of "eating" his body and "drinking" his blood, will come to the fore. Interestingly, the pastry "*sarcophagus*" from *Babette's Feast* is a powerful Eucharistic reference, inasmuch as the word is based on two terms we will hear in the weeks ahead (*sarx* = flesh, *phagein* = eat). May all Christians, who trust in Christ as they eat his flesh, make their own the prayer after Communion: "Accompany with constant protection, O Lord, those you renew with these heavenly gifts and, in your never-failing care for them, make them worthy of eternal redemption. Through Christ our Lord."

"Laying Down Your Life"

Acts 4:5–12; John 3:16–24; John 10:11–18

Pastor Jana Schofield
Christ Lutheran Church
Ferndale, Washington

IN ITS CONTENT, ARRANGEMENT, and language usage this sermon exemplifies many of the items discussed in the text. The introduction, interesting in itself, clearly functions as a bridge from the gospel reading to the substance of the sermon. While exhibiting depth of thought, the sermon is made interesting with a wide variety of supporting materials including quotations, a personal narrative, and illustrations. Her references to Luther, Bonhoeffer, and Bishop Hanson are relevant, concrete, and specific. Can her listeners forget her call to discipleship, to "suffer with others"? The word *suffers* or *suffering* appears thirty-four times as the sermon's theme is repeatedly applied to the listener. The conclusion illustrates the effective use of questions as it ends a coherent sermon with clear direction by relating back to its beginning references to the Good Shepherd.

Laying Down Your Life

Dear friends in Christ, Grace and Peace to you from God our Creator, Christ our Savior, and the Holy Spirit who dwells among us. Amen.

There was a little girl in church who was learning the Twenty-Third Psalm that begins, "The Lord is my shepherd, I shall not want." Instead, she said, "The Lord is my shepherd, that's all I want." I think maybe she has the best translation—that's all we should want, because in reality, that's the most important thing we need. I need the Lord as my shepherd, the good shepherd, who as we heard today, lays down his life for the sheep. I'm fascinated how many times in this gospel text from John Jesus talks about laying down his life:

I am the good shepherd. The good shepherd lays down his life for the sheep.

I know my own and my own know me . . . and I lay down my life for the sheep.

I lay down my life in order to take it up again.

No one takes it from me, but I lay it down of my own accord.

I have power to lay down my life, and I have power to take it up again.

Jesus laid down his life, to the point of death, for us. For you. For me. And the second scripture lesson we heard today from the first letter of John explains why: "We know love by this, that Jesus Christ laid down his life for us." Jesus laying down his life is how we comprehend the love of Christ for the world.

And that letter of 1st John continues: "We know love by this, that Jesus Christ laid down his life for us—and we ought to lay down our lives for one another. How does God's love abide in anyone who has the world's goods and sees a brother or sister in need and yet refuses to help?" Little children, let us love, not in word or speech, but in truth and action.

We ought to be laying down our lives for one another . . . it is the call to being a disciple of Jesus. But what does it really mean to lay down our lives? I believe that discipleship, following Jesus, means that we see, that we suffer, and that we serve.

I got glasses for the first time about seven years ago while I was in seminary. I have one eye that is near sighted and one eye that is far sighted, so for my entire life up to that point my brain was always switching off one eye whether I was seeing near or seeing far. When I put on corrective lenses for the first time so that both eyes worked together I remember that I saw depth, corners, and sharpness like I had never seen before and I remember thinking—oh, *that's* what's really out there in the world! Being Christian and laying down our lives means that we receive a new set of lenses that make us say—oh, *that's* what's really out there in the world. And what is out there in the world is a whole lot of suffering. Jesus had that lens, and it constantly propelled him into situations where there was suffering, grief, sickness, and death.

I think some Christian churches use Jesus Christ not as a lens with which to see the world but rather as a shield between them and the world. They are so concerned with Paul's exhortation to not be of the world that they don't even heed his call to be in the world. Jesus never called us to avoid the world, because the world is where we are needed. But what Jesus did call us to do was to be attentive to the world like the Good Samaritan was to the man who was robbed and beaten on the side of the road.

Seeing means paying attention to the suffering that is right there in front of us and usually bypassed by the rest of the world. Theologian Douglas John Hall says this: "If the church does not *see* this suffering and then, seeing it, does not take the burden of it upon itself, then its whole life must be called into question." If we, Mt. Carmel Lutheran Church, are not attentive to the suffering of the world, then we aren't understanding what it means to lay down our lives: (from 1st John) "How does God's love abide in anyone who has the world's goods and *sees* a brother or sister in need and yet refuses to help?"

It may not be easy to hear this, but it's true: the call to discipleship is the call to suffer—not because suffering is good or beneficial or ultimately rewarding, but we are called to suffer because there *is* suffering in God's world. As Paul puts it, "The whole creation groans." In the church we learn what it means to have compassion—the word which comes from the Latin *compassio* which means "to suffer with." As Christians, we requisitely have compassion for the world—we suffer with a world in pain.

Martin Luther listed suffering among the marks of the church—if a church does not suffer with the world, then it has become untrue to its destiny. Do you remember Martin Luther's definition of sin? "Cor incurvatus en se"—the heart curved in on itself. In contrast to sin, then, faith is what changes our vision from looking inward to looking outside ourselves—toward the friend who knocks on our door at midnight in need, toward the people of the Gulf Coast as they continue to recover from hurricanes, to the thousands around the world who are dying each day for lack of food, water or medical care, toward Darfur and Angola and Iraq and Israel and Palestine.

The church is a community of suffering because it is a community whose eyes have been opened to the suffering that exists. Of course, Jesus knew this more than anyone. Not only were Jesus' eyes open to suffering, not only did Jesus lay down his life on the cross, but while he was dying on the cross, he was still giving his life away. He was conscious of the pain of others—of the thieves on either side of him being crucified, of his followers who were standing beneath the cross, devastated. He suffered himself and yet had compassion, suffered with those in pain. Yes, we all suffer too, in our own accord—to be human means that we will suffer—there is no way to avoid some suffering in life. But that doesn't mean that we can give up our call to discipleship by saying, "I'm suffering so much myself—I can't give anything." Laying down our lives first means being attentive to others' suffering, which has the benefit of putting our own suffering in perspective, and then joining in the suffering of others.

Dietrich Bonhoeffer, the great Lutheran German theologian during World War II said, "The Christian must therefore plunge himself or herself into the life of a godless world, without attempting to gloss over its ungodliness with a veneer of religion or trying to transfigure it. He or she must live a 'worldly' life and so participate in the suffering of God. It is not some religious act which makes a Christian what he or she is, but participation in the suffering of God in the life of the world."

When Lutheran pastors are ordained, we make a promise, a vow, to seek justice on behalf of the poor and oppressed. When our confirmation students are confirmed in two weeks, they'll be making a promise to serve all people, following the example of our Lord Jesus, and to strive for justice and peace in all the earth. It is the natural next step after we see a world in suffering and suffer with it that we serve a world in suffering. We prayed it today in the prayer of the day: "Send us as shepherds to rescue the lost, to heal the injured, and to feed on another with knowledge and understanding." We are not true to our Christian faith if we do not follow what we see in the world with a commitment to serve the people in it who are suffering. Again that question from 1st John: "How can God's love abide in anyone who has the world's goods and sees a brother or sister in need and yet refuses to help?"

My dad is in Jerusalem and Bethlehem again right now for a board meeting of the Lutheran schools in Palestine. He emailed me on Friday about the conversations he's been having with Palestinians who, though innocent and trying only to live their daily lives, are under tremendous economic and psychological distress because of funding cut off to their government and their confinement by the Israeli separation wall. Augusta Victoria Hospital, the Lutheran World Federation Hospital on the Mount of Olives and the only hospital in the Holy Land which serves Palestinians in need of kidney dialysis and some cancer treatments, is in dire financial crisis because the Palestinian government has had to eliminate its funding. Our ELCA bishop Mark Hanson wrote about the situation in this months' Lutheran magazine, saying, "Church, find your voice"—find your voice, your prayers, your wallet, your compassion to suffer with and to serve "the least of these."

How can you find your voice? How can you lay down your life, this afternoon, this week, this year? How can you see, suffer with, and serve a friend in need and a world in pain? How can you be a shepherd to sheep who need the Good Shepherd? I pray that you leave here today asking those questions, remembering that the Lord is *your* shepherd, you shall not be in want, and you have what you need to serve God's people. Amen.

"Devotion for the Resurrection"

John 20:1

Bishop Jerry L. Ogles, DD
St. Andrews Anglican Orthodox Church
Enterprise, Alabama

BISHOP OGLES' RESURRECTION SERMON was preached on Saturday, the day before Easter Sunday. As preface to an argument he wishes to make, the pastor takes special note of the gospel text stating that Mary Magdalene came to the tomb early, "when it was yet dark." A case is then made for the possibility that the resurrection may have occurred on Saturday evening, although that distinction is viewed as a "nonessential" in relation to the essential beauty and significance of Easter.

The introduction not only introduces the gospel text, but introduces Bishop Ogle as a teaching pastor. Portions of the sermon included here exemplify his teaching style which is characterized by clear explanations undergirded by relevant biblical texts. With reference to the value of going beyond the lectionary text for the day, Pastor Ogle employs seven additional references from John's account, along with references from 1 Peter and Mark, and five references from Matthew's gospel.

A good example of Bishop Ogle's teaching style is found at the end of the sermon, in what he calls a postscript to the central theme surrounding Mary Magdalene and the resurrection. "Much ado," the pastor says, is made of Peter's place in the church, so the bishop explains the ambiguity regarding the name Peter by distinguishing between *Petros* and *Petras*.

The best teaching comes from those who can see below the surface to reveal new knowledge or give new meaning to what we have known only superficially. In his "postscript" Bishop Ogle does this in an insightful way as he goes beyond the surface of the simple statement, ". . . tell his disciples, and Peter." Following his description of Christ's great concern and compassion for Peter, the pastor applies all of that to his listeners as he assures each one of the love and grace that is brought to us in the Easter resurrection.

It is the thoughtful study of the Word and the contemplation of its meaning that brings to life the power of the Word, as Bishop Ogle has done so brilliantly, yet so simply and so well.

Devotion for the Resurrection

We observe the resurrection of Christ in all its glory at this time— perhaps a day early, but we should always check our road maps of Easter before we launch out into the deep. It is not altogether inappropriate to undertake the observance of Christ's resurrection on Saturday as it could very well have happened on Saturday evening as the Sabbath began to dawn toward the first day of the week. "In the end of the Sabbath, as it began to dawn toward the first day of the week, came Mary Magdalene and the other Mary to see the sepulchre" (Matt 28:1). I will remind the reader that the "end of Sabbath" always occurs at sundown on our Saturday. One thing is certain from the text: Christ did not arise at sunrise on Sunday as some churches promote in their sunrise services. It was yet dark when Mary Magdalene came to the tomb. But those are the nonessentials. The essential beauty of Easter is that Jesus did rise from the Garden Tomb.

"Mary stood without at the sepulchre weeping: and as she wept, she stooped down, and looked into the sepulchre, and seeth two angels in white sitting, the one at the head, and the other at the feet, where the body of Jesus had lain. And they say unto her, Woman, why weepest thou?" (John 20:11–13). Mary had come to find a dead body which she loved more than life, but she was in for a surprise. When the angels looked at poor Mary standing without the tomb, they could see behind her as well. They could clearly see the figure standing behind Mary. They must have been exultant with joy! "She saith unto them, because they have taken away my Lord, and I know not where they have laid him" (John 20:13). The dead and missing body of a beloved Friend and Savior is certainly cause for weeping. But she persisted in trying to determine the body's whereabouts—and she soon would!

"And when she had thus said, she turned herself back, and saw Jesus standing, and knew not that it was Jesus" (John 20:14). How many times have we been troubled about being alone without Christ when He stands just before us! The profuse tears of Mary blinded her in the same way as those of Hagar did by the Fountain of the Wilderness. She saw Jesus, but he seemed very blurry through the tears. She mistook Him for the Gardener! But do you know what? Jesus IS the Gardener and Giver of Life! "Jesus saith unto her, Woman, why weepest thou? Whom seekest thou? She, supposing him to be the gardener, saith unto him, Sir, if thou have borne him hence, tell me where thou hast laid him, and I will take him away" (John 20:15).

There was nothing in the voice to alert her to the Personage with whom she spoke even though the words of Jesus were precisely the same as that of the angels. The Lord may often surprise us with joy at finding Him where we think not. But no one can call your name as Jesus does. It is sharp and distinct and different from every other voice. Even the dead body of Lazarus at Bethany responded to his name being called forth by Jesus. "Jesus saith unto her, Mary. She turned herself, and saith unto him, Rabboni; which is to say, Master" (John 20:16). Once Jesus had called Mary's name, there was no need for further explanation. Once He calls your name, you will know and respond, too. No one could call Mary's name with the same love, tenderness, and authority. Her tears of mourning turned into tears of absolute joy! That is what Christ does for the poor sinner, and for those whom He has called. What a blessed Easter morning was this! Mary became the first messenger to deliver the fullness of the Gospel of the risen Christ. "Mary Magdalene came and told the disciples that she had seen the Lord, and that he had spoken these things unto her" (John 20:18).

Postscript: There is much ado made about Peter as the Pillar Stone of the Church. That is a Roman misinterpretation. The Rock upon which the Church is built is Jesus Christ. Peter (Petros) means "small stone." Petras, by which Christ makes reference to Himself, means large Rock. Indeed, Christ is the Rock, and Peter (and you and I) are chips off that Rock if we belong to Christ. Peter himself makes adequate distinction: "Behold, I lay in Sion a chief corner stone, elect, precious: and he that believeth on him shall not be confounded. Unto you therefore which believe he is precious: but unto them which be disobedient, the stone which the builders disallowed, the same is made the head of the corner" (1 Pet 2:4–7).

But there is a great point that I want to make about Peter. As you recall, Peter has denied Christ three times the night of His trial. He is the only disciple to have so egregiously done so. He has not distinguished himself by his actions. He is bitterly pained at having done so, and at having Christ turn and look him in the face on his third denial. He wept bitterly, and must have suffered tremendous regret. I hope you will consider what the angels said to the women gathered at the tomb: "But go your way, tell his disciples and Peter that he goeth before you into Galilee: there shall ye see him, as he said unto you" (Mark 16:7). I hope you noticed the particular reference to Peter when when referring to the other disciples and—"and Peter." God is no respecter of persons, and this was no honorific in mentioning Peter's name specifically. I believe the cause was that the Lord knew what Peter had suffered over the past hours. He knew the anguish in Peter's heart as he wondered if he had so offended and disgraced his sovereign Lord that there could be no rapprochement with his Lord. Even at such a time, the love of Christ for His own is evidenced in the angel's message to "the disciples and Peter." Our Lord takes particular regard for us, too, not because we are special human beings in His service, but because He knows our every weakness and still loves us dearly in spite of our warts and weaknesses. He loved us enough, not only to die for our sins on Good Friday, but to defeat death and Hell in His Easter resurrection for us. Do you glory in that thought?

Amen

"God Is In This Place"

Genesis 28:16

Rabbi Alissa Wise
St. John's Presbyterian Church
San Francisco, California

RABBI WISE'S SERMON WON the 2012 Hossana Preaching Prize awarded by the Israel/Palestine Mission Network of the Presbyterian Church in the USA. Partly because of its length, but also because the entire sermon is readily available on the web, only the beginning portion is included here.

Rabbi Wise begins with a reference to the Genesis account of Jacob's awakening at Bethel, then through an extended narrative the speaker draws the analogy to her own awakening, to the presence of God in the planting of trees, in the constructive work she is doing.

The sermon is replete with vivid, image-arousing language which contrasts the historic Jewish values of justice, equality, and peace with a current scene where Rabbi Wise speaks of violence, brutality, illegal expansion, blatant injustice, oppression, and daily humiliation.

Rabbi Wise turns to historic Jewish traditions to support her central argument that wrong doing needs to be addressed. She introduces and defines the word *tochecha*, the concept of sacred rebuke, a part of the Holiness Code, the section of the Torah which focuses on moral and ethical imperatives. In further support of the concept of rebuke, Rabbi Wise quotes from a third-century rabbi,

Yossi ben Chanina, "A love without reproof is no love." The rabbi also makes it clear that *tochecha*, rebuke, must be grounded in love and respect.

An overview of the complete sermon presents a speaker who builds on her own ethos in the initial narrative and adds to it in the knowledge and attitude she evinces throughout. The sermon depends heavily on pathetic proof, the appeal to traditional Jewish values, but there is also an underlying logical appeal in both the *tochecha* affirmation and in the argument implicit in contrasting the current West Bank scene to traditional Jewish values. Rabbi Wise's conclusion applies the tochecha as an obligation for her listeners: "Now we must face the test of our own integrity."

Contemplating this sermon brings my mind all the way back to first-century BC Rome and Cato's definition of a great orator as "a good man speaking well."

God Is In This Place

In Genesis we read: Jacob woke from his sleep and said, surely God is in this place, and I did not know it!

It happened for me like that too. Well, maybe not exactly. Let me tell you what happened.

In the summer of 2007, while I was studying to become a rabbi, I lived in the West Bank for two months. One day I planted trees in a destroyed olive grove outside of Nablus. I was working with local Palestinian farmers and a group of activists from Sweden. None of the Swedish activists were Jewish; most of them were anarchist college students who were on the first trip to the Middle East, there just for a couple of weeks to support Palestinian non-violent resistance.

Before we set out for the day, we exchanged information in case of arrest or injury, chose individuals to negotiate with the army, and reminded each other to follow the lead of the Palestinian farmers, to retreat when they wanted to and not to stray from the group.

As we walked the four miles out to the plot of land where the olive trees had been uprooted and now would be replanted, we got to know each other a bit. The Swedish internationals were intrigued that I was becoming a rabbi, and on our long walk out to the grove, they questioned me about what I believed about God. As happens a lot when I am with anarchists and activists who don't like or trust organized religion, there was skepticism, or at least a confusion about my religiosity; especially as the nearest religious Jews were the ones who did the uprooting. I would often dodge the question about God in this kind of situation.

But, at that moment I had an answer. As if, I, like Jacob suddenly woke up. There I was on the lookout for Israeli military snipers or jeeps and being pressed to answer what I believed about God, in a land full of claims on God. I scanned my history—my family's connections to Jerusalem, my teen camping trips in the north of Israel, my dance club days in Tel Aviv in college—and I came to truly understand for the first time that it was against all odds that I was standing there. I had planted trees not too far from Nablus before with the Jewish National Fund—before I knew of their participation in the erasure of Palestinian history. Yet there I was, a middle-class American Jew raised in a right-wing Zionist Jewish home, and now I was helping Palestinian farmers plant trees as an act of resistance in the occupied West Bank. It was in response to this question asked of me in Nablus that I filled in the blank about God. God is the impulse in me to serve the Other out of a sense of responsibility that stems from the Source of redemption.

God was in this place and I did not know it.

And, then I did. I never looked back.

"What Is to Prevent?"

Act 8:26–40

John Rollefson, Interim Pastor
Bethania Lutheran Church
Solvang, California

IN ADDRESSING THE EMOTIONALLY loaded, highly controversial topic of the acceptance of LGBTQ persons into full fellowship in the Christian church, Pastor John Rollefson allows the Word to speak for itself. The sermon illustrates the perspicacious employment of an inductive arrangement to approach an important topic which to some parishioners was still controversial and troubling.

Traveling the path of an extended narrative, the journey takes the listener from one positive scene to another, building an affirmative response at each step: Philip is warmly invited to share the VIP's carriage. Philip's scriptural knowledge is welcomed. Baptism is eagerly accepted. The eunuch goes on his way rejoicing. As the narrative unfolds from one affirmation to another it creates both a logical and psychological predilection to affirm the conclusion.

As you will readily discern, Pastor Rollefson is very much a teacher. Beyond the basic necessities of dealing with the text, there is a great deal of material which enriches the sermon and makes it especially interesting. There is, for example, information about Philip, about the Mediterranean world, about Gaza, both as a word and as a place, and about the role of the eunuch in that society. There are also several "asides" which suggest the speaker was keenly aware of his audience as he made personal connections, such as his reference to the text from Luke, "I love it." On Philip's initial query to the eunuch, Rollefson's personal observation is that he hears a note of condescension, even racism in Philip's voice. As he envisions the image of Philip and a black VIP reading scripture while seated in a luxurious carriage, he shares his own questioning as he wonders why so few artists have painted the extraordinary scene. These personal comments and insights add interest and may contribute to the speaker's ethos.

This sermon is, clearly, a person speaking.

What Is to Prevent?

Throughout this Easter season our first readings have all been taken from St. Luke's writings, what we call the "Acts of the Apostles." We've been led through a series of stories in which the Spirit of God is depicted as "wafting" those earliest Christians into ever new situations, presenting them with ever more challenging opportunities to "practice resurrection" in ever new circumstances of life increasingly remote from the old orthodoxy centered in Jerusalem.

The Spirit in today's first reading from the 8th chapter of Acts gusts the mission of the early church in the direction of opening up new frontiers for the Gospel on a number of fronts, breaking new ground "*geographically, racially,* and *sexually.*"

The story is one of the most exotic and picturesque in all of the New Testament. I love it! It begins, as so many of Luke's stories, with an angel—a messenger of God—who directs Philip, one of the earliest Christian leaders, who because he possessed a Greek name (the same name as Alexander the Great's father) probably spoke and read the Greek language—the *lingua franca* of the eastern Mediterranean world—like English today, perhaps.

"*Get up and go toward the south to the road that goes down from Jerusalem to Gaza,*" the angel says, and Luke supplies the footnote as an aside ("*This is a wilderness*"—or maybe better—"*desert road*"—not a lot of traffic, in other words). Our ears prick up, don't they, because Gaza is a place of contemporary political significance—the Gaza Strip, we say, which is that stretch of land handed over some years ago by the state of Israel to the Palestinian Authority, dotted with the remains of some of the most wretched refugee camps in the world where Palestinians have languished for more than sixty years now—along that desert stretch of land along the Mediterranean that even now as then was where the road to Egypt lay—the symbolic connecting link between Asia and Africa.

It is to this desert road that Philip is directed by God's angel, "*so he got up and went,*" the text simply says—no ifs, ands, or buts. And what did Philip find on this remote desert road? Luke takes painstaking care to describe what Philip found, piling up one adjectival phrase on top of another in his eagerness to detail the scene for us.

"*And behold,*" Luke writes, Philip caught sight of *an Ethiopian eunuch, a court official of Candace, queen of the Ethiopians, in charge of her entire treasury.* (Now the biblical Greek word for "treasury" is "gaza," the same word as the place where this event is happening.) This Ethiopian eunuch, Luke goes on to tell us, "*had come to Jerusalem to worship and was returning home and was seated in his chariot, reading the prophet Isaiah.*"

Luke gives us seven highly descriptive phrases to set this exotic scene, so let's pay some attention to the details of the story.

The man Philip encounters is, first of all, an Ethiopian, which most certainly means a black-skinned African from the remote region in the Upper Nile south of Egypt itself—what today we call the Sudan.

Secondly, this man is a *eunuch,* Luke tells us, which means, bluntly, a castrated male, sad to say but in the ancient world it was a fairly common phenomenon which was thought to guarantee the trustworthiness of a servant or slave put in charge of a nobleman's womenfolk. The word "eunuch" in Greek literally means "guardian of the bedchamber." We'll be returning to this in a bit.

Thirdly, this Ethiopian eunuch, we're told, was a court official of the queen of the Ethiopians. No lowly servant this, but Luke further explains, he was the minister in charge of the queen's "gaza," her treasure, her secretary of the treasury, a very prominent person, a VIP, in other words.

But next we learn that this Ethiopian eunuch minister of finance of the queen had come to Jerusalem to *worship*—not as part of a trade delegation nor on a political junket nor as a tourist—but to *worship*, and now he was returning home, on his way home from a "pilgrimage" we might call it.

Further, we learn from Luke that he was seated in a chariot. Only the richest of the rich had horses, much less chariots, perhaps the equivalent of a stretch limo today.

And finally, Luke tells us, last but not least, he was sitting there in his chariot reading the prophet Isaiah—maybe the oddest detail of them all—probably meaning Isaiah in its Greek translation called the Septuagint, scholars speculate. Remember there weren't any Gideon Bibles that he could've picked up during his stay in the Jerusalem Hilton. This must've been an expensive scroll of the prophet that he had somehow been able to obtain.

Now these last details make us particularly curious for we can't help but wonder, was this Ethiopian eunuch interested in becoming a Jewish convert—a proselyte as the Jews call them—or was he just a seeker after religious truth curious about the Jewish faith? Maybe some of you will remember how some years back there began an Israeli resettlement effort of black Africans from Ethiopia who claimed to be Jews from ancient times who'd kept the Jewish faith for centuries while living in Ethiopia.

Or maybe—we don't know for sure—this prominent Ethiopian eunuch had somehow heard the rumor about this new sect within Judaism that was so agitating the temple establishment in Jerusalem—a group that simply called itself "The Way" and followed an itinerant Galilean by the name of Jesus of Nazareth who had been summarily crucified by the Romans a few Passovers ago, and whose followers claimed had been raised from the dead as God's Messiah. We don't know the answers to these questions with any certainty, but they're intriguing, aren't they?

All we're told is that the Spirit, like a following wind, had swept Philip into an encounter with this exotic traveler, saying,

"Go over to this chariot and join it." So Philip ran up to the chariot where he heard the man reading the prophet Isaiah and inquired (I can't help but hear a note of condescension, maybe even racism, in his voice): *"Do you understand what you're reading?"* To which the man in the chariot replies without missing a beat, *"How can I unless someone guides me?"* The Greek literally says, "How can I unless someone shows me 'the way'"—again, a kind of pun, I suppose, since "the way" was the early church's way of naming itself. And so, just as we encountered Jesus "opening the minds of the disciples to scripture" that first Easter night in the Emmaus story, so here too Philip is invited to "show the way" into understanding Scripture for this African seeker after truth. *"And he invited Philip to get in and sit beside him."*

So now—get this. Picture this scene in your imagination as Luke has so painstakingly painted it for us. I wonder why so few artists of biblical scenes—a Michelangelo or Titian or Rembrandt—haven't risen to the challenge of depicting this wonderful scene: a Greek-speaking Jew and a well-dressed black African eunuch sitting side by side on a chariot seat parked on a desert road reading together the scroll of the prophet Isaiah. A pretty bizarre scene for the occasional camel driver passing by, wouldn't you say?!

The passage the man in the chariot was reading, Luke bothers to tell us, just happens to be from that well-known 53rd chapter of Isaiah, the one we last heard read on Good Friday, from one of the so-called "suffering servant songs" that the infant church very early on began to interpret in the light of Jesus' death and resurrection: *"Like a sheep he was led to slaughter and like a lamb silent before its shearer . . ."* And so, when the man in the chariot asks Philip with great politeness, *"About whom, may I ask, does the prophet say this, about himself or someone else?"* the man has presented Philip with a natural opening to share with him the good news of Jesus—the answer to this and all his questions—as Philip, like his Master Jesus before him, began to "open his mind" to the true meaning of Scripture, the good news of Jesus Christ.

"And as they were going along the road," Luke says—for apparently this had now become a conversation on the move, literally

"on the way"—they came to some water—perhaps an oasis?—and the eunuch exclaimed to Philip, *"Look here is water! What is to prevent me from being baptized?"* An awfully good question, don't you think, to which, apparently, Philip had no good answer. For *nothing* was to prevent his being baptized, and so the Ethiopian yelled, "Whoa!" stopped the chariot, and he and Philip jumped into the water together, and Philip right there and then baptized the Ethiopian eunuch finance minister of the queen—right there and then, without even a "new member class." Philip just did it at the man's urging and, the story concludes, as they came up out of the water Philip was literally "spirited away"—*"the Spirit of the Lord snatched Philip away,"* Luke says. And the newly baptized Ethiopian eunuch finance minister of the queen saw him no more, the text says, as he went *"on his way rejoicing"* as we sing in the words of the old hymn.

It's a wonder-full story isn't it—literally a story to *"wonder at."* It's a story that pushes out the frontiers of the church—geographically, racially, sexually. It is particularly to the last of these frontiers that I'd like us to focus our attention this morning. For having introduced to us with those seven highly descriptive phases our exotic central character, Luke then goes on *four* times to refer to the man simply as "the eunuch." Among all his distinguishing characteristics, his sexual condition was the one by which Luke chose to label or identify him. Notice, for everything else we know about him, we do not know his name.

Why might this be significant? I think, first of all, is the fact that according to Deuteronomy 23:1, Jewish law formally excluded eunuchs, castrated males, from the company of the faithful at worship. Eunuchs, like other blemished, defective and disabled minorities were categorically excluded from full participation in the covenant community, never mind that most eunuchs were not responsible—but were rather victims—of their emasculation and their subsequent condition.

But secondly, I can't help but wonder if one of the reasons that the eunuch of the story was found by Philip reading the 53rd chapter of the scroll of the prophet Isaiah may not also have been because in chapter 56 of Isaiah—a short three chapters later—a few turns of the scroll—we find these welcoming words written of the messianic kingdom of which Isaiah prophesied:

> *Thus says the Lord:*
> *"Keep justice, and do righteousness,*
> *for soon my salvation will come*
> *and my deliverance be revealed."*

And then in verse 3:

> *Let not the foreigner who has joined*
> *himself to the Lord say,*
> *"The Lord will surely separate me*
> *from his people":*
> *and let not the eunuch say,*
> *"Behold I am a dry tree."*
> *For thus says the Lord:*
> *"To the eunuchs who keep my Sabbaths,*
> *who choose the things that please me*
> *and hold fast my covenant,*
> *I will give in my house and within*
> *my walls a monument and a name*
> *better than sons and daughters;*
> *I will give them an everlasting name*
> *which will not be cut off."*

And then, finally, skipping down to verse 8 in words that to my ears sound remarkably similar to the words we heard the Good Shepherd Jesus utter last Sunday when we heard Jesus say, "*I have other sheep who do not belong to this fold. I must bring them also, and they will listen to my voice.*" Isaiah writes:

> *Thus says the Lord God,*
> *who gathers the outcasts of Israel,*
> *"I will gather yet others to him*
> *besides those already gathered."*

Sisters and brothers in Christ, the welcome of eunuchs into the church is not the issue on the frontier of the Gospel's mission toward sexual minorities in our day. But you know what is, and thank God our church, the ELCA after years of painful turmoil has answered the question of the Ethiopian eunuch, "What is to prevent?" with a resounding, "Nothing is to prevent."

May we the church learn to practice resurrection in our welcome and acceptance as the Spirit continues to waft us onto ever-new frontiers of mission. For Christ is risen! Christ is risen indeed! Alleluia. Amen.

"The Floodgate of Grace"

Readings: Wisdom 7:7–11; Psalm 90:12–13, 14–15,
16–17; Hebrews 4:12–13; Mark 10:17–30

Deacon Peter Lovrick
St. Augustine's Seminary
Toronto, Ontario

IN THIS HOMILY THE listener is immediately drawn into the narrative of the Gospel text and made to feel the discontent of the rich young man and to share his troubled and puzzled thoughts as he goes away. There is a solution to the apparently inexplicable problem and the speaker provides his listeners a "heads up" as he tells them that within that solution there is an important message that needs to be heard. "That message is . . ."

The homily then proceeds to explain, define, and apply the concept of God's grace, and to clearly explain its relation to good works.

Is this Monroe's motivated sequence: Attention-Problem-Solution-Application? Probably not intentionally, but the clarity in that problem-solution pattern contributes to the clear direction and focus this homily sustains throughout its presentation.

The Floodgate of Grace

If you squirm in your seat when you hear Jesus tell us today what it takes to inherit eternal life you are *not alone. I squirm, too. It is not enough, it seems, to keep all the commandments; as if we could even*

99

do that well. Oh, no. Even if we were to keep all the commandments, follow all the rules, never miss Mass—as Jesus said to the
young man, it is still not enough because one thing is lacking: "Go
sell what you own, and give the money to the poor, and you will
have treasure in heaven."

What are we supposed to do with that?! If you're not St.
Francis of Assisi or St. Clare, who both did just that, your sympa-
thies might lie with the young man who goes away grieving. You
might have a lot in life, you might not—but if we are better off
than impoverished refugees, people trapped in war—we can't help
but imagine Jesus looking right at us, and then, maybe, squirm
in our seats. Okay, sure, we can donate something now and then,
help out, we aren't heartless. But what Jesus asks of the young man
today is too much.

And you might be tempted to just think to yourself: "Well,
that's not going to happen," and just dismiss the whole thing. Maybe we'll get a nicer Gospel reading next week. We can be tempted
to do that because it's all so unreasonable, even impossible.

But to do that is to miss a very important message in this
Mass that needs to be heard. That message is that Jesus agrees with
us: it is impossible for us. So impossible that it is as ludicrous as a
camel going through the eye of a needle. The disciples themselves
despair: Who can be saved? Who can keep all the rules, and sacrifice themselves so totally for others?

And Jesus gives them the answer. What is not possible for
people is possible for God. It is possible for Jesus. It is Jesus himself, who is God, who will follow all the rules, do the Father's will.
And it is Jesus himself, who is God, who will sacrifice himself so
totally— giving everything he has, even his life.

That opens the floodgate of grace for you and for me. It makes
our salvation possible. That is why the opening prayer of this Mass
declares that God's grace, at all times, goes before us, and follows
after us. What Jesus did accomplishes what is not possible, and
enables us, the prayer says, to carry out good works.

The good news of this Mass is that we do not have to go away
grieving like the young man. We don't have to tune out the message

either. We can embrace the gift of God's grace that says, of course, we could never earn our salvation on our own. As if we could follow the rules, do all the right things, and then somehow God would owe us. The Church defined that as a heresy centuries ago.

Far from it. Our yearning for God is grace, what we do for God as our response to him is grace, and whatever we do in cooperation with God bears fruit because of grace.

Our good works have merit, but it is God's grace that saves us, and enables those good works in the first place.

That is why in 1999, *The Joint Declaration on the Doctrine of Justification by the Lutheran World Federation and the Catholic Church* was issued resolving a bitter misunderstanding between Catholics and Protestants.

The declaration proclaimed the truth of the Church that: Together we confess: By grace alone, in faith in Christ's saving work and not because of any merit on our part, we are accepted by God and receive the Holy Spirit, who renews our hearts while equipping and calling us to good works.

And then it proclaimed: We confess together that good works—a Christian life lived in faith, hope and love—follow justification and are its fruits.

Christ has won us that grace. He gives it to us in our baptism, and we drink deeply of it in the sacraments. That is why we are here. That is why we will approach the altar to receive that grace in the body and blood of Christ. And that is why the prayer after Communion will declare that God nourishes us so that we might become sharers of his divine life. That we might inherit eternal life after all—and not have to go away grieving.

We go away, not grieving, but rejoicing, in the words of the psalmist, for what God has done for us, and for what he has invited us to:

Fill us with your love, O Lord, that we may rejoice and be glad.

"God's Easter Shout of Victory"

1 Cor. 15:54; John 10:10

Pastor Fred Meuser
Lamb of God Lutheran Church
Haines City, Florida

THE ENERGY AND EXUBERANCE, the positive spirit of this Easter sermon is implicit in language consistent with the theme, "God's Easter Shout of Victory." Listeners can identify with the joyful jumping and hugging that follows a victory on the playing field and the pastor quickly moves that spirit to the joyfulness of Easter.

The portions of the sermon included here illustrate both contrast in language usage and contrast in the development of the victory theme. The language ranges from plain and direct, even earthy, to the gospel texts and to the beautiful words of the hymns sung that day. The development of the victory theme employs both affirmation and negation, with the yes and the no in sharp contrast.

This sermon is a clear example of preaching by *proclamation*, and preaching with reference to multiple biblical texts. Because Pastor Meuser is a retired seminary president, one might say that ethical proof is a natural ingredient of this presentation. It is also a sermon that both challenges and encourages the listener with the authority of the scriptural text.

God's Easter Shout of Victory

How do athletes celebrate great victories? Tennis champions collapse on the ground. Baseball players pile in a heap on top of the winning pitcher. Football players pour gallons of Gatorade onto the head of their coach. Fans jump, hug, and exchange high fives. Victory time is a celebration time!

Easter is victory time supreme. You know our victory cheer: *The Lord is Risen! He is Risen Indeed!* Easter is shouting time for us, because it is shouting time for God! And God's Easter Shout of Victory is *"Yes!"* A resounding *Yes.*

Early in his life, many people said *yes* to Jesus. They loved His miracles and begged for more. He was the talk of the town. The people were spellbound by what He was saying. But the more He spelled it out, the louder the *Nos* became.

And when they they saw Him hanging like a butchered steer on the cross arm of a pole, all of them, except His mother and a few other women, felt like the disciples on the road to Emmaus: "And we had thought He was the promised Messiah." One more disappointment, one more shattered dream . . . "One more fraud." He talked such a good game, but look what has happened . . .

Not a fraud, this Jesus, not a pretender, not an unrealistic dreamer. But the real thing, the genuine article. *Yes!* My Beloved Son! Look at Him! Listen to Him! Follow Him! Easter doesn't mean seeds produce flowers, or caterpillars butterflies, or life is stronger than death, love stronger than hate, or that we "all go to a better place" when we die, or any of the other watered down clichés that rob this incredible event of its true meaning. It means, first of all, full endorsement of Jesus, everything about Jesus, by His Father.

Read the New Testament with God's *yes* about Jesus in mind:

I am come to bring your life abundant (Jn 10:10)—*Yes!*

Let anyone who is thirsty come to me and drink
(Jn 7:37)—*Yes!*

Love one another as I have loved you (Jn 15:12)—*Yes!*

Blessed are the merciful and the peacemakers
(Matt 5:7, 9)—*Yes!*

I am the Way, the Truth, the Life (Jn 14:7)—*Yes!*

Except you repent, take up your cross and follow me you cannot be my disciple (Matt 16:24)—*Yes!*

Heaven and earth will pass away, my words, Never
(Matt 14:35)—*Yes!*

His countrymen said *No.* Religious leaders, *No.* Roman government, *No.* The crowds, *No.* The disciples, *No.* Even one of the thieves hanging on the cross beside Him, *No.* Lots of people today say No, or I don't care.

But God, by raising Him from death, shouted *Yes!* To every word, every act of compassion, every tear, every pain. And on every moment of Jesus' life from Bethlehem to His ascension, God stamped *Approved! Perfect! Authentic! Endorsed! Vindicated! Guaranteed! Validated! Certified!*

But there is more to God's Shout of Victory than *Yes.* Strange as it may seem, God's Shout is also *No!* How can it be both *Yes* and *No*? To what did God say *No!* when Jesus rose from the dead?

You know there was much more to Jesus' life than telling stories, performing miracles, suffering and dying. From manger to cross to resurrection Jesus' life was also a war against the evil that sinks its claws into us, that poisons us and the whole world. To that evil and to its evil father, Satan, God in Jesus' resurrection say *No, You Are Not In Charge Of This World!* It does not belong to you, no matter how it may look . . .

At the very start of Jesus' ministry, Satan in the wilderness says to Him, "You don't have to go through all this suffering and dying business to win followers. Just guarantee them good meals and a comfortable place to live. And if you assure them of a good retirement you'll have to fight them off with a stick! Or you can *Wow* them with a leap off the temple steeple to a soft landing 400 feet below! Just recognize that my way is more effective than yours." Jesus' answer? A firm straight-arm to the chin: *No Way! No!*

So when St. Paul asks, "What can we say to all this?" we can say with him, "I am sure that nothing in death or life . . . nothing in the world as it is or as it shall be, nothing in all creation will ever be able to separate us from the love of God . . . in Jesus Christ our Lord."

That's why just before this sermon you heard the choir:

Sing to the Lord a song of praise

A Wonderful marvelous song!

And why in a moment, we'll all sing

Thine is the glory, risen, conquering Son

Endless is the Vict'ry, Thou o'e r death hast won!

So how about our Victory Shout one more time?

The Lord Is Risen! He is Risen Indeed! Alleluia!

"The Outrage"

Luke 4:21–30

Pastor Stuart Schadt
Trinity Episcopal Church
Manassas, Virginia

THE OCCASION OF JESUS' return to Nazareth presents a difficult text which Pastor Schadt insightfully uses to challenge his congregation to a fresh understanding of God and of themselves. The sermon calls us to identify with the congregation in Nazareth who were "filled with rage" and responded in anger at the message Jesus brought to them.

The sermon introduces specific, real-life situations to which the listener can easily identify, instances where we might be outraged by the acts or words of others. The instances are used to challenge the listener to embrace conflict, to learn to see our neighbor, ourselves, and our God in a new way. We are asked to create new possibilities, to learn new truths.

The conclusion relates directly back to the introduction which imaginatively raises the question: What might those people of Nazareth have received if just one of them had put anger to rest and calmly inquired, "What do your words mean? Why have you come?"

The Outrage

He is asked to read . . .

The young man enters the congregation. There are whispers among the worshipers.

"Have you heard what he did last week?"

"Everyone is talking about it."

"He sure has grown."

"Aren't those his parents?"

"Isn't his father the carpenter?"

He is asked to read from the scroll and he reads a prophecy from Isaiah. Then he takes a seat. All eyes are on him. He says, "This day these words are fulfilled in your hearing." They are astounded. No one else speaks with such authority, such certainty. And if that is not enough he goes on. He says that the great deeds he has done elsewhere he will not do here. Were there not many hungry widows in the days of Elijah and did he not feed just one. And were there not many lepers in the days of Elisha and did he not only cleanse Naaman.

These words sent the congregation into a rage. They drove him from the building to the edge of town where they were ready to cast him over a cliff. But he turned and passed through the midst of them.

There are several explanations about why these words that Jesus spoke so enraged this congregation. Some say the people were angered because he would not do for them the miracles he had done for others. I think, though, he challenged their understanding of their relationship with God. He challenged their place as God's chosen people. And that challenged their understanding of God and their understanding of themselves. Rather than confront the possibility of a new vision, they would drive from themselves the messenger.

It is true that sometimes people come into our lives, even into our spiritual lives, and into our churches and say things to us that we find outrageous. They say things that cause us to rage.

When I went to seminary back in the mid-seventies I had done some Bible reading; in fact it was reading the Bible that brought me into an active adult relationship with God and with the church. I had taken a few Bible courses as electives in college. Our New Testament professor was Dr. Reginald Fuller, a renowned New Testament scholar. Early in the semester he let us know that the only words of the Gospel that he was certain were a direct quote of Jesus, accurately recorded was "Abba," the word that we translate as "Our Father" at the opening of the Lord's Prayer. Abba is an Aramaic word of relational intimacy that might be better translated as Papa. What Dr. Fuller meant by this claim was that every other word attributed to Jesus had been spoken by Jesus in Aramaic, remembered by his apostles, then translated and written down in Greek.

Well, I found this teaching troubling but some of my classmates found it outrageous. We lacked any cliffs nearby, but I think they would have gladly thrown our professor off a building.

Back in the late sixties when the church was going through a tumultuous time there were such credible threats against the life of Presiding Bishop Hines that the national church hired body guards to protect him. All because what he said and what he did was found by some fellow Episcopalians to be outrageous.

When some people first encountered altars moved away from the wall, or women priests or people of color as priest, some people found this outrageous. I know that when I was at the microphone I said things that others found to be outrageous. There were no cliffs nearby but there were balconies, but we did not drive anyone from the room or over the balcony.

Why do we find these things to be so outrageous? I think they are challenging our understanding of God, our understanding of our relationship with God, and our understanding of ourselves, and rather than work with all that, we just want to drive it away. Shut it out. But what if we don't drive it away or shut it out?

Maybe if we can put aside our rage and risk the encounter, maybe we will know God in a new and different way. Or maybe, and this is just as valid, we will be reaffirmed in the truth we already know, but we will know our neighbor in a new way.

I understand and I preach God as a loving, inclusive, forgiving God. But the scriptures we read also tell me of God as wrathful, vengeful, and exclusive. While it is tempting to only read those scriptures I like, to do so would short change me and my faith.

I am sorry that people come into our lives and into our church and say outrageous things. I am sorry that at times I have said and done things in church that people find outrageous. But if it were not so then it would mean that we were all in the same place and we all agreed. And soon our faith would grow stale and then small and then maybe die.

Go back with me now to that synagogue in Nazareth where Jesus came to speak. After Jesus spoke a few short sentences, they drove him out. Think of what in their raging anger they missed. Think of what gifts they might have received if one person could have put aside their rage and said, "Tell us more. What do your words mean? Why have you come?"

Preaching Thoughts
re: the Holy Spirit

I LOVE THE WORSHIP service in all its parts. The Word in prayer, music, and liturgy culminates in the preaching of the Word. The preaching can be an incarnation here and now, every week: An encounter with God, the Word made flesh in its application to real people . . . the Word, equipping the worshipping community for mission and service in their everyday lives.

I admire the ELCA statement *The Use of the Means of Grace.* Even though I would urge clergy to keep in mind its brief but perspicacious section on preaching, I nevertheless disagree in part with its definition of preaching, i.e. "Preaching is the living and contemporary voice of one who interprets in all the scriptures the things concerning Jesus Christ."

In our church our God is a triune God. In our songs, our liturgy, and in our sacraments the trinity is reflected in a balanced way. In our preaching it is not. God the Father receives some attention; God the Son receives nearly all the rest. The third part of the Trinity, God the Spirit, receives almost none.

Dominus Est? Is it the Lord? Does not everyone yearn for God's presence? Did not Christ pray that as he goes to his heavenly father, the Holy Spirit would then take his place here on earth with them? Is not Christ here with us now in the Holy Spirit, as councilor, teacher, and comforter? In this world is it not the Holy Spirit which brought understanding to the disciples? In this world is it not through the Holy Spirit that we experience Christ's presence in us, a presence that brings joy to a Christian life? Do we not pray, "Renew a right spirit within me . . . and take not thy spirit from me?" And is it not the same Holy Spirit which empowered the disciples at Pentecost which now empowers the Christian life as we abide in him and he in us?

Christ tells us that apart from his Spirit in us, we can do nothing. By contrast, with the Spirit we exhibit love, joy, peace, patience, kindness, generosity, faithfulness, gentleness, and self-control. So, let's hear it for the Holy Spirit, and not just on Pentecost Sunday.

Sabbatical Leave Policy

PURPOSE: FOR THE CHURCH, the purpose is to strengthen its ministry. For the clergy person the purpose of such a leave is for spiritual, physical, and intellectual renewal. The application for leave must be consistent with these intentions and must indicate how the applicant intends to achieve specific goals consistent with the general purpose of renewal.

Eligibility: Following the completion of five years of service in the present call, a sabbatical leave may be granted to ordained clergy serving the congregation. Once the sabbatical is completed, the five-year service period begins anew before the clergy person is eligible for the next sabbatical.

Conditions of Leave:

1. A sabbatical leave may be for a minimum of three months and a maximum of six months, with full compensation for a three-month sabbatical and half compensation for a six-month sabbatical. Other time periods will be compensated proportionately.

2. Regardless of the period of leave, the applicant for a sabbatical is urged to seek outside grant funding for the purpose of (a) providing replacement funds for his/her ministry and (b) for special expenses of the sabbatical plan such as books, tuition, or travel.

3. Sabbatical leave should be planned to be the least disruptive to the life of the church. Specifically, plans should avoid Easter and Christmas if possible and should include summer

months unless the regular academic year is essential to the sabbatical plan.

4. The leave application will be submitted in writing to the personnel ministry team no later than six to twelve months prior to the beginning of the proposed leave, depending on budget planning requirements. While applicants should feel free to creatively develop their individual plan, such plans may include formal study at a seminary or university, a period of clinical pastor education, independent study, travel, or a combination of these. When the leave proposal is endorsed by the personnel ministry team, it is then forwarded to the congregational council for approval.

5. The clergy person taking the leave will submit a written leave report to the congregational council within thirty days of completion of the leave. The acceptance of a sabbatical leave carries with it the commitment to return to the position for at least a full year or to reimburse the church for its costs for the leave. Such reimbursement shall be due thirty days after the completion of the leave, or at the time the position is vacated prior to the fulfillment of the one-year commitment.

Dialogue on Stewardship

The Lord speaks to us:	We speak to the Lord:
Give of the first fruits. Exod 23:19 Prov 3:9	We offer with joy and thanksgiving what you have first given us . . . ourselves, our time, and our possessions. LBW Liturgy, 67
You will know them by their fruits. Matt 7:16	
If any of you want to be my followers, let them deny themselves, take up their cross daily, and follow me. Luke 9:23	With them [our gifts] we offer ourselves to your service and dedicate our lives to the care and redemption of all that you have made. LBW Liturgy, 68
Truly I tell you, this poor widow has put in more than all those [rich] who are contributing . . . for all of them have given out of their abundance, but she out of her poverty. Mark 12:41–44	We give thee but thine own, whate'er that gift may be. All that we have is thine alone, a trust, O Lord from thee. LBW Hymn 410
He who sows sparingly will also reap sparingly. The Lord loves a cheerful giver. 2 Cor 9:6–7	We joyfully return to you what you have first entrusted to us. May these gifts be signs of our whole lives offered to you, dedicated to the healing and unity of all creation. Now the Feast and Celebration Liturgy. 10.

The Lord speaks to us:	We speak to the Lord:
As you did to the least of these my brethren, you also did to me. Matt 25:40	You who made the heavens splendor, every dancing sun of light, make us shine with gentle justice, let us each reflect your light. Service of Light Liturgy, 13.
Do not be conformed to this world. Rom 12:2	This Is My Father's World, LBW Hymn 554

Bibliography

Aristotle. *Rhetoric*. Translated by Rhys Roberts. New York: Modern Library, 1954.

Bassett, Lee Emerson. *A Handbook of Extemporaneous Speaking*. Ann Arbor, MI: Edwards, 1927.

Bonhoeffer, Dietrich. "Sermon on 2 Cor. 12:9." In *Dietrich Bonhoeffer: A Biography*, by Eberhard Bethge, edited by Edwin Robertson, translated by Eric Mosbacher et al., 505–11. Minneapolis: Augsburg Fortress, 2000.

Bono. Keynote address, 54th National Prayer Breakfast, Washington, DC, February 2, 2006. http://www.americanrhetoric.com/speeches/bononationalprayerbreakfast.htm.

Brooks, David. "The Next Culture War." Op-Ed, *New York Times*, June 30, 2015.

Burke, Kenneth. *Counter-Statement*. Berkeley: University of California Press, 1968.

———. *The Philosophy of Literary Form: Studies in Symbolic Action*. New York: Vintage, 1957.

Campbell, George. *Lectures on Pulpit Eloquence*. London, 1824. Internet Classics Archives, University of Michigan.

Cox, James, ed. *Best Sermons 6*. San Francisco: Harper, 1993.

DePalma, Michael-John, and Jeffrey M. Ringer, eds. *Mapping Christian Rhetorics: Connecting Conversations, Charting New Territories*. New York: Routledge, 2015.

Endres, David J. "The Mystery of the Trinity." *Homiletic & Pastoral Review*, May 2015.

Evangelical Lutheran Worship. Minneapolis: Augsburg Fortress, 2006.

Foer, Joshua. *Moonwalking with Einstein: The Art and Science of Remembering Everything*. New York: Penguin, 2011.

Frost, Gerhard E. *Blessed Is the Ordinary*. Minneapolis: Winston, 1980.

———. *Deep in December: Meditations on the Later Years*. Visitation Pamphlet series. Inver Grove Heights, MN: Logos, 1986.

———. *It Had Better Be True: Reflections on Death and Resurrection*. Visitation Pamphlet series. Inver Grove Heights, MN: Logos, n.d.

Grace-full Use of the Means of Grace: Thesis on Worship and Worship Practices. Edited by Gordon Lathrop et al. North American Academy of Liturgy, 1994.

Haugen, Marty. *Service of Light*. A liturgical service. Chicago: GIA, 2015.

Johnson, W. R. "Isocrates Flowering: The Rhetoric of Augustine." *Philosophy & Rhetoric* 9 (1976) 217–31.

Loscalzo, Craig A. *Preaching Sermons That Connect: Effective Communication through Identification*. Downers Grove: InterVarsity, 1992.

Lovrick, Peter. "Preaching the Homily and the New Evangelism." *Homiletic & Pastoral Review*, June 2015.

Lutheran Book of Worship. Minneapolis: Augsburg Fortress, 1978.

Monroe, Alan. *Principles and Types of Speech*. Madison, OH: Foresman, 1949.

Nichols, Marie. *Rhetoric and Criticism*. Baton Rouge: Louisiana State University Press, 1963.

Nouwen, Henri. *Out of Solitude: Three Meditations on the Christian Life*. Notre Dame: Ave Maria Press, 1986.

Plato. *Phaedrus*. Translated by Benjamin Jowett. Internet Classics Archives, MIT. http://classics.mit.edu/Plato/phaedrus.html.

Richards, I. A. *The Philosophy of Rhetoric*. London: Oxford University Press, 1965.

Sayler, Robert N., and Molly Bishop Shadel. *Tongue-Tied America: Reviving the Art of Verbal Persuasion*. New York: Wolters Kluwer, 2011.

Sheen, Fulton J. "The Virgin Who Is a Mother." Sermon. Catholic Hour Broadcast, January 21, 1951.

Sittler, Joseph. *Gravity and Grace: Reflections and Provocations*. Minneapolis: Augsburg, 1986.

Strunk, William, and E. B. White. *The Elements of Style*. 3rd ed. New York: Macmillan, 1979.

Taylor, Barbara Brown. *An Altar in the World*. New York: Harper Collins, 2009.

The Use of the Means of Grace: A Statement on the Practice of Word and Sacrament. Minneapolis: Augsburg Fortress, 1997.

Valentine, Tim. "Finding God at the Heart of Things." *Homiletic & Pastoral Review*, July 2015.

Wells, Sam. "Turning All into Alleluia." Sermon preached at the Duke University Chapel, September 4, 2011. Published in *Faith & Leadership,* September 19, 2011. https://www.faithandleadership.com/samuel-wells-turning-all-alleluia.

Winans, James A. *Speech-Making*. New York: Appleton-Century, 1915.

Index

Index